5265

ROCKLIN, CALIFORNIA
95677

RICHARD COSTIGAN

The Book of Low-Fire Ceramics

The Book of Low-Fire Ceramics

by Harvey Brody

Photographs by
David Powers

Holt, Rinehart and Winston/New York

First published in January 1980 by Holt, Rinehart
and Winston, 383 Madison Avenue, New York,
New York 10017.

Published simultaneously in Canada by Holt,
Rinehart and Winston of Canada, Limited.

Library of Congress Cataloging in Publication Data

Brody, Harvey.
    The book of low-fire ceramics.

    Bibliography: p.
    Includes index.
    1. Pottery craft. I. Powers, David.
II.Title. III. Title: Low-fire ceramics.
TT920.B78 1979   738   79-944
ISBN Hardbound: 0-03-042116-0
ISBN Paperback: 0-03-042111-X

First Edition

Designer: Brenn Lea Pearson
Printed in the United States of America
10 9 8 7 6 5 4 3 2 1

For my Mother and Father
For Kay

and all the other sweet talkers, good-night kissers,
magicians, and pyrotechnicians

There walks the Boar at Beauty's side
Swollen with Desire
    Lo, the blushing earth abides
    Lo, the wind
    Lo, fire.

              —*Medieval love song,*
                 author unknown

Contents

Color photographs fall between pages 74 and 75.

Acknowledgments

The Book of Low-Fire Ceramics is really the outcome of the experience of putting a book on low-fire ceramics together. New information and new ideas as well as new experiences kept changing the shape of the book as I pursued my original outline. There was a lot of hard and intense work to make the book happen, but not until I learned to *let* it happen did the pieces fall into place. One of the original falling pieces was David Powers.

When I first met David, I told him my vague notions about wanting to photograph people working in their studios making low-fire ceramics. So we started to work and I discovered that even though David had not been around ceramics studios very much, he picked up instantly on rhythms, moods, and details during the shooting. All the important things, I realized, to help capture the experience of what we were watching. And David was really interested in what he was seeing, cared enough to ask questions without interfering with the work at hand. All the principals involved were amazed and thankful for his unobtrusiveness. Which meant we all had a lot of good times together, talking about ceramics, photography, past lives, and aspirations. David helped make the project one of the few that hasn't bothered me because it kept me from my own studio.

Then there are those people whose lives David and I walked into to photograph. Without their enthusiasm, concern, and graciousness, the thrill really would have been gone and it would've shown. We spent a lot of time with Richard Shaw, Will Herrera, David Middlebrook, Duane Ewing, and Bill Abright; and with Dan Oberti, Leonard Skuro, and Wilson Burrows.

Many thanks to Pauline Ammirata for her patient help. And to the American Art Clay Company, Robert Brent Corporation, the Quay Ceramics Gallery, the Hansen Fuller Gallery, the Institute of Ceramic Phenomena, Phil Eagle, and the Meyer Breier Weiss Gallery.

And special thanks to Bill Henkin, who sweet-talked me into doing this book in the first place and whose keen editorial and directorial talents never intruded on our friendship.

Foreword

Hardly a season passes without a major art gallery or museum launching a new show of ceramics. In the past few years, in fact, a number of galleries have devoted themselves to showing *only* works done in clay. Much of this work has the hard edge and brilliant color we've come to expect more from the space-and-plastic age than from the earthier traditions of pottery. Hobby ceramicists and industrial ceramicists have been using these low-fire colors and sheens for years, yet they have only recently been discovered by the studio artist and craftsman.

In the past, "art pottery" or sculpture was associated more with large factories or companies than with the individuals who did the work. But in the 1950s and 1960s, many people working in clay, particularly those artists now labeled "abstract expressionists," made the transition from "pots" to "objects," helping to establish ceramics as a recognized and recognizable art form.

The use of low-fire techniques became a popular method of furthering that objectification and blurring the memory of clay as a utilitarian medium. It opened the door to a more painterly approach to ceramics by offering the ceramicist a broad and intense palette of colors and highly predictable results. Soon the galleries were filled with toilets, frogs, bananas, '49 Studebakers, Pepsi bottles, entire living rooms, and other articles of our collective consciousness, striking crisp poses in their new clay roles. We continued to recognize the medium though, even dressed in its Saturday-night flash, because *whatever* the *object*, clay remained the *subject*.

Low-fire ceramics has developed very rapidly at the studio level, in conjunction with a highly sophisticated approach to form and decoration. What once appeared as garish and brash has been toned down and refined and can now be understated. Low-fire is now acceptable and commonplace. And students want to know how to do it. So do many craftsmen who have been working in high-fire; some are beginning to do their utilitarian pottery using all or a few of the low-fire processes. So, in a sense, a cycle completes itself: the low-fire techniques first used by a few studio artists have been popularized and pushed back into the general acceptance and use whence they came. The result has been a broadening of the state of contemporary ceramics—fewer restrictions and fewer definitions, more things *seem* possible. The gallery work need not always inspire your imagination or spur you on to create apocalyptic pottery. What it does do is create an easier and more expansive atmosphere in which to work.

The advantages of low-fire as opposed to high-fire are considerable from a practical point of view. There is the obvious reduction in fuel consumption—it takes less energy to reach lower temperatures. In addition, the space and mechanical requirements for setting up a low-fire studio are much less than for a high-fire studio. The low temperatures can be reached with electric kilns easily set up in home basements or garages. The gas kilns usually required to reach high temperatures, particularly for reduction firing, entail all sorts of plumbing, venting, regulatory permits, and, basically, a home of their own. If the scale of work is reduced, a person can maintain a small studio for a nominal capital outlay.

Fast Foreword

Let me say straight off that this book hardly exhausts the subject of low-fire ceramics. I wouldn't want that distinction, since it would mean admitting that there is a stagnant body of knowledge that comprises all there is to know about low-fire. Since techniques and processes become individualized and used and combined in an infinite number of ways, the subject expands with each person's experience. One cannot write a definitive study of literature by listing the alphabet and rules of grammar. Thus I have tried to make *The Book of Low-Fire Ceramics* more than an alphabet, to show that the *experience* of a process is as important as the process itself. I wanted to relate my own experience with clay, to communicate the many years of joy and frustration.

There are many other places to gain information and many other ways to experience clay. It's no secret that the ceramics industry has been using low-fire processes for hundreds of years and by now has a vast technical knowledge stored away in thick dull books. Because industrial requirements are so different from those of an individual artisan, the results are too rigid and unexciting for most of us. One method promotes a science of predictable products, while the other looks for the unpredictable and a more relaxed way of working. Yet this vast body of knowledge can be of great technical help in solving problems created by the imagination.

The Book of Low-Fire Ceramics is made up of two distinct parts: the text and the photoessays. Much of the textual material has been simplified to make it accessible to the beginner as well as the professional. I have concentrated on the subjects that are relevant solely to low-fire processes, although keeping in mind that low-fire is only a special condition of ceramics in general. Thus, throughout the text and in the bibliography, I have recommended other books that might be of some help in obtaining further specific information or insight.

The photoessays stand as both an extension of the text and in opposition to it. They deal with more advanced material, either not covered or barely covered in the text. At the same time, they picture five people who often break the rules established by the text to pursue their creative endeavors. The photographs are not meant to glorify their processes, but to portray their experiences, to show the willingness of these people to make mistakes and venture a little further than they have gone before, based on their own instincts and past knowledge. It is this spirit of working that seems important to me: to be bold enough to push your luck and sensible enough to learn from your mistakes.

The photoessays are as much concerned with the life force, the personal rhythm behind the pieces, as they are with demonstrable information. None of the photographs in the essays are setups; they depict real people working amid a lot of personal clutter, surrounded by personal symbols and important and unimportant memorabilia. Looking at someone else's toolbox is as informative as learning how to mix plaster. The idea is not to teach you how to make a Richard Shaw plate, but to show you how Richard Shaw incorporates and integrates various techniques into a personal way of working. You don't necessarily want to be a frog after watching one jump off a lily pad, nor do you have to make frogs with your clay in order to have benefited from seeing that jump.

How-to books always make me think of frogs laid out and dissected in an anatomy class. Even with the snappy rhymes and ditties (the kneebone's connected to the legbone, the legbone's connected to the footbone, and so on), what you've got is a dead frog in front of you. It seems to me that had I not seen a frog jump or heard it go croak in the night I would have missed the reason for cutting it open in the first place.

Harvey A. Brody
Healdsburg, California

The Book of
Low-Fire Ceramics

1

The Clay's the Thing: Low-Fire Clay Bodies

Regardless of what you *think* you know about clay, you really know a lot more. Because much of this book deals with technical information and rational explanations, I want to tell you at the outset that working with clay is a very intuitive process. I want to remind you of what generations of school kids were not and still are not taught in "Ceramics" or "Pottery" classes, since they know instinctively what to do with a piece of clay: roll it and smash it—because it doesn't break—and then form it into a seven-legged dinosaur ashtray or super-duper rocket explorer ship or maybe just a flat giant apple. So whether you've been making things out of clay for twenty years or are just starting, there is something this book can't teach you; you already know it.

For most of us, the first experience with clay is very disjointed; we have no idea of a complete process. Maybe you were one of those kids making dinosaur ashtrays, or maybe you just saw some finished pieces and said to yourself, "I'd like to do that," without knowing what that meant. You may be at that very stage now, and these first few paragraphs are intended to serve as your simple introduction to the complete process and to the magic that transforms clay from a soft and pliable lump to a hard and permanent, if often fragile, object. Watching clay transform itself *is* like magic, and no matter how much you learn about clay, the magic remains.

To effect a change in clay, from soft to hard, requires heat. No matter what you do with clay, how you form it, decorate it, or glaze it, you have to give it up to the *kiln* (a heating chamber) and take what comes out after the heat is applied. You cannot physically be inside the kiln directing things, holding legs onto bodies or handles onto cups. So before you put them into the kiln, you need to know what effects heat will have on the clay pieces. The more experience you have, the less risk you take. The fire change is the part of the clay process that is least under our control and the one that most often leaves us in the dark.

Understanding the importance of heat leads to understanding why things made of clay can be divided into two major categories: high-fire ceramics and low-fire ceramics.

These two simple groupings are distinguished one from the other by the *amount of heat applied* to a piece of clay to make it hard and durable. In low-fire we use less heat to obtain a hard state than we use in high-fire.

Some Basic Clay Language

First, you should become conversant with a few terms and conventions concerning heat.

1. The process of heating a kiln is called *firing*; the ceramics taken from the kiln are said to be *fired*.

2. Temperatures inside kilns are measured by *cones*. A cone is a small piece of clay formulated to melt at a specific temperature during a specific rate of firing. Cones are used inside kilns rather than, or in addition to, mechanical devices, because they give a more accurate indication of what actually happens to a given clay or glaze in the firing process as a result of

both *time* and *heat* (see chart, opposite). A mechanical device that is sometimes used to get approximate temperatures while firing but is more useful determining temperatures while a kiln is *cooling*, is called a *pyrometer*. Most clay and glaze notations are made in cone numbers instead of temperatures. For example, for the purposes of this book, and somewhat arbitrarily, I am designating anything fired below cone 1 low-fire. The really dramatic characteristics of low- and high-fire ceramics become apparent well above and well below this arbitrary mark. The bright primary colors and the gold and silver lusters occur between cone 020 and cone 06, while the true porcelains and celadons happen above cone 8.

3. Every clay has a specific *melting point*. Since this phrase refers to the temperature at which clay turns to liquid and makes a mess of our fondest illusions, it is more convenient, and better suited to our needs, to refer to the *maturation point* of clay. The maturation point is the temperature at which a clay develops its maximum hardness and nonporosity before it begins to melt and distort.

Taking It Apart

Most of the clay that exists on earth is of the low-fire variety. This is due to the large quantities of iron oxide and other mineral impurities that mix with the clays in their natural states and lower their maturation points. In other words, we can differentiate between that which *is* clay and that which *affects* clay when mixed with it and fired.

When geologists use the word *clay* they are usually referring to *kaolinite*, a mineral made up of thin, flat hexagonal crystals, and having a theoretical formula $Al_2O_3 \cdot 2SiO_2 \cdot 2H_2O$. It is a naturally occurring substance created by the disintegration of

ORTON STANDARD PYROMETRIC CONES AND THEIR TEMPERATURE EQUIVALENTS[a]

Cone number	Large cones		Small cones	
	150°C[b]	270°F[b]	300°C[b]	540°F[b]
020	635	1175	666	1231
019	683	1261	723	1333
018	717	1323	752	1386
017	747	1377	784	1443
016	792	1458	825	1517
015	804	1479	843	1549
014	838	1540		
013	852	1566		
012	884	1623		
011	894	1641		
010	894	1641	919	1686
09	923	1693	955	1751
08	955	1751	983	1801
07	984	1803	1008	1846
06	999	1830	1023	1873
05	1046	1915	1062	1944
04	1060	1940	1098	2008
03	1101	2014	1131	2068
02	1120	2048	1148	2098
01	1137	2079	1178	2152
1	1154	2109	1179	2154
2	1162	2124	1179	2154
3	1168	2134	1196	2185
4	1186	2167	1209	2208
5	1196	2185	1221	2230
6	1222	2232	1255	2291
7	1240	2264	1264	2307
8	1263	2305	1300	2372
9	1280	2336	1317	2403
10	1305	2381	1330	2426
11	1315	2399	1336	2437
12	1326	2419	1335	2471
13	1346	2455		
14	1366	2491		
15	1431	2608		

[a]from the Edward Orton, Jr., Ceramic Foundation, Columbus, Ohio
[b]temperature rise per hour

feldspathic rock. Yet ceramicists deal with hundreds of different types of clays that seldom appear in a pure form. But it is useful to conceive of clay as that pure mineral state, somehow changed or added to by the geologic forces of the earth, even though technically we know how our clays have been altered, and how such alterations change their applications.

Historically, pottery makers were usually limited to whatever local clays were handy. Since low-fire clays were available extensively, and since the technology required to obtain low-fire temperatures was minimal, most pottery was low-fire. Today, because of advanced technology, we no longer have to resign ourselves to local clay deposits that don't fully meet our needs and demands; yet ironically, this same technology may prevent us from reaching high temperatures in the near future because of the rapidity with which we are depleting our fossil fuels.

A *clay body* is simply a mixture of clay or clays and whatever other materials it takes to create the qualities of workability and the fired results desired. If you think your clay will work better with shredded Argyle socks in it, they should become part of your clay body. Sometimes, though, a single, common red clay will have all the properties necessary for use in the studio, which makes your clay-body formulation very simple.

For low-fire work, the first requirement, of course, is that the clay body have a maturing temperature in the low-fire range, around cone 1 or below. There is no good or bad firing range; there is only what works or doesn't work for you. Your own needs, then, must dictate what cone you fire to. Suppose, for example, you can buy a commercially prepared clay body which the manufacturer suggests firing to cone 06, but you know of a terrific cone 1 glaze that simply can't be reproduced at a lower temperature.

Clay bodies often have a wide firing range—four or five cones—which allows for flexibility in firing. So the first thing to do is to try firing the clay to cone 1 and see what

happens. In fact, the higher temperature may increase the strength of the clay and produce nicer pieces. (If the clay body melts or deforms at cone 1, use the information to be found later in this chapter to formulate your own body.) Clay manufacturers will always play it safe in making firing recommendations. In order to determine the real limits of a clay body, you must push it to those limits. Find out what it can or can't do by testing it. Knowing how to change a clay formula allows you to pick up where Providence left off.

The materials used in low-fire clay bodies fall into these four classifications:

1. Clays

2. Fluxes

3. Grogs and Fillers

4. Colorants

Start with the real stuff—clay, or a blend of clays—and make any necessary additions to it.

Clays

When crushed fine enough, clay becomes plastic when wet, and permanently hard when fired to its maturing temperature. We can classify all clays loosely on the basis of *color, refractoriness*, and *plasticity*.

We can refer to *color* in the raw unfired clay, but we are more concerned about it in the fired state.

Refractoriness is the quality of resisting heat.

Plasticity is a loose, subjective term that refers to the ability of a clay to change its shape readily. Whether or not a clay is plastic enough for your own particular forming process is a question you need to answer on your own. Most ceramicists perform a small ritual when they confront any new clay body. They roll out a coil of clay between their hands and bend it in a full circle. If the coil neither cracks nor splits, the clay is considered to be plastic. If it does crack or split, it is said to be *short*. Obviously, these terms are applied relative to one's experience with clay. For good results—results that will satisfy you, and on which you can rely—you should extend your test beyond a preliminary feel. Use the clay. Do whatever you have to do to determine whether it is helping you or hindering you.

Clay that is too plastic will shrink excessively and will tend to crack while drying. You can remedy an overly plastic body by adding a nonplastic material such as kaolin or grog (see below), although adding any material other than a grog or filler will alter the maturation point of a clay body and may affect the glazes. You can increase plasticity by adding a very plastic clay, such as *ball clay* or *bentonite*, or by inducing bacterial growth in the clay. Additions of beer, old clay, vinegar, or starch encourage the proliferation of bacteria. White or green mold will begin to form on the clay following the addition of any such material, and the clay will begin to smell musty. These are all good, healthy signs. Aging clay always helps to plasticize it, theoretically because water has a better chance to soak in and thoroughly wet all the particles. It should only take a week before a clay that has been mixed from dry materials is thoroughly wetted.

China Clay or Kaolin

These are usually *primary* or *residual* clays, which means they have remained on the site of the rocks from which they were formed. As a result of the geological formation process, they are fairly pure and free from contamination. Thus kaolins are an indispensable source of pure white clay. At the same time, these clays are coarse, not overly plastic, and very refractory, maturing around cone 34 (3182°F, 1750°C).

There are also *sedimentary* kaolins, such as the common *EPK* from Florida, which have been transported by water from their parent rocks. As a result of their travels, they are finer-grained and much more plastic than primary kaolins.

Ball Clay

These are *sedimentary* or *secondary* clays, which have been transported by wind or water and redeposited before becoming associated with organic matter, although it is the organic matter that imparts the dark color to unfired ball clays. The organic matter will, however, burn out completely when fired. Ball clays are very fine-grained and highly plastic, and therefore shrink a good deal. An excess of ball clay—more than 60 percent of a clay body—can cause drying cracks and warping. Most ball clays are very refractory and require fluxing agents for use in low-fire. Their fired colors range from white to dark gray.

Fire Clay

This name encompasses many types of refractory clays that do not have the purity of kaolin or ball clay. Fire clays vary in plasticity and color, so testing is in order for any local fire clay you might find. A light-burning fire clay may suffice for an off-white low-fire body. Fire clays are generally less refractory than kaolins but more so than earthenware, and will require some fluxing agent for use in low-fire.

Earthenware Clay

These are the high iron-bearing clays most common in nature, and most useful in forming nonwhite low-fire clay bodies. In their natural states they come in all colors: red, brown, green, gray, yellow, and even blue. It is not difficult to find some local red earthenware clay for testing. A brickyard might be willing to sell you some of the clay it uses. Be forewarned, however, that brickmakers usually rely on a very coarse and sandy clay whose plasticity is very low.

Bentonite

This is a clay derived from volcanic ash whose mineral constituent is *montmorillonite*. It is very plastic and therefore shrinks a good deal.

It can add plasticity to a clay body, but more than 2 percent may create cracking and warping problems because of the high shrinkage rate associated with any highly plastic material.

Pyrophyllite

This is one of nature's weirdos. It has physical properties similar to *talc*, and a crystalline structure like montmorillonite; yet is nonplastic. It is a useful material because of its low *coefficient of expansion*. This means it doesn't shrink much when fired and retards the shrinkage of the body it's in, thus making the body more resistant to sudden temperature changes, such as those experienced by ovenware.

Fluxes

The essential difference between a high-fire and a low-fire clay body is the amount or strength of flux associated with each. A *flux* is a material that causes or promotes melting in a clay because of its own very low melting point, thus making the body more vitrified and durable. The iron oxide associated with earthenware clays, for instance, not only acts as a colorant, but also as a flux. Fluxes include *feldspars*, *nepheline syenite*, *frits*, some colorant oxides, and *talc*. All fluxes are nonplastic and therefore do not improve the working properties of a clay, unless it is already too plastic.

Frits

Frits are substances that have been melted together, cooled quickly by immersion in cold water, and then ground to a powder. This process renders some materials into more usable forms. For example, *lead oxide* may lose its high toxicity after it has been fritted with silica. Fritting allows us insoluble forms of otherwise soluble materials, such as *boric oxide*, B_2O_3. Frits themselves are slightly soluble and may cause deflocculation of the clay

(see chapter 2) and make it impossible to work with. It's unlikely, however, that frits will cause such drastic problems, and since they are such strong fluxing agents it is well worth the minimal risk. Because of the numerous leadless frits on the market, there is no need to use lead, even in a fritted form, in low-fire clay bodies.

Talc

Talc is the major source of flux in low-fire clay bodies. It maintains the whiteness of a body, and has a long firing range. It is also relatively inexpensive. Some talcs, especially from California, contain asbestos, so it is important to protect yourself from any dust raised when using talc as a dry ingredient. Talc is a nonplastic material whose fluxing action is not as great as most frits. The results of absorption tests on clay bodies I've tested, shown further on in this chapter, point out that the standard white body of 60 percent ball clay and 40 percent talc is not as vitrified or strong as bodies using other fluxing agents, either alone or in association with talc.

Feldspars

Feldspar is an igneous mineral that makes up about 60 percent of the earth's crust, and is the parent of almost all our clays. Feldspars are usually a mixture of *aluminum silicates* ($Al_2O_3 \cdot SiO_2$—recall kaolinite), sodium, potassium, calcium, and lithium. Most feldspars are denoted as either *soda spar* or *potash spar*, depending on whether the percentage of sodium (soda) or potassium (potash) is higher. *Nepheline syenite* is the usual choice for fluxing low-fire clay bodies, since it is much more active in the lower firing range than normal feldspars. It is composed of nepheline, microcline (potash feldspar), and albite (soda feldspar).

Wollastonite

This is a fibrous *calcium silicate* mineral, $CaSiO_3$, that has a very low coefficient of expansion, which decreases the fired shrinkage in a body and makes it less susceptible to heat shock (see page 11). It will produce a light beige tint in a fired clay body.

Lithium Compounds

Lithia, LiO_2, when used as a body flux will also reduce firing shrinkage rates and increase shock-resistance because of its low coefficient of expansion. Spodumene, lepidolite, petalite, amblygonite, and lithium carbonate are all sources of lithia.

Eutectics

There is a phenomenon working in our favor when we attempt to lower the firing ranges in clay bodies by the use of fluxes. We know that every material we are using has a melting point, or temperature at which it starts to liquefy and help vitrify the clay. However, it sometimes happens that when two materials are mixed and heated together, the resultant mixture melts at a temperature lower than either of the components would alone. For example, the melting point of lithia, LiO_2, is about cone 32 (1700°C), and that of silica at its lowest is cone 17 (1470°C). A composition of 55 percent silica and 45 percent lithia will melt near cone 06 (1024°C). This mixture is called a *eutectic composition*.

Sometimes three components produce even more radical results. So the possibilities of using fluxes are greatly extended with the use of eutectic combinations in our search for a denser, more vitrified clay body at the lower temperatures. Lists of eutectic compositions are published in most industrial textbooks if you want to pursue the subject. In any case, you should be aware of the phenomenon when formulating and testing clay bodies.

Grogs and Fillers

Grogs are materials with comparatively large particle sizes used to "open" a clay body and reduce shrinking, cracking, and warping.

Technically grog is clay (often in the form of bricks) that has been fired and ground up. Grogs are usually screened and sold by mesh sizes: the smaller the number, the coarser the grog. The screen size refers to the number of openings per square inch on a screen. A 30-mesh grog, then, was screened through a 30-mesh screen, and everything that was left on the screen was *not* included in that batch of grog. Most commercially available grogs are 60 mesh, a medium-fine grain, but coarser and finer grains are available.

Fired grogs are of large particle size compared with the rest of the clay body, and because they don't undergo any further shrinkage themselves, they help to reduce the amount of shrinkage in any body they're added to. This helps prevent warping and cracking. Grogs are nonplastic but can add a great deal of working strength to a clay body. Large pieces, for instance, really need the "bones" that grog provides in order to stand while wet. And if a piece has walls thicker than 3/8 inch (approximately 1 centimeter), it is almost essential to use some kind of grog in the body.

For an earthy red clay body, the rough texture imparted by the coarser grogs may be appealing and desirable. In whiteware, however, it may interfere with the overall design, particularly if the surface of a piece is to be graphically detailed. Fine-grained grogs, such as the one used for high-fire porcelain called *molochite*, are available in white. One of the viable alternatives to grog is *sand*, especially pure silica sand. This can be added, like grog, to make up 20 percent by weight of a clay body. The amount of grog or sand used is determined by the method of forming and the strength requirements. The more grog used, the less plastic the resulting clay body, and generally, the weaker it becomes in the fired state.

Some of the more fascinating pieces being done these days are results of finding grog substitutes. For example, one of the popular additives is *expanded plaster aggregate*. It is available at most plant nurseries under the trade names Alvalite, Zoolite, and Perlite.

They are the little white dots you see in planting mixtures, which nurseries use to break up and aerate soil. An addition of 20 percent by weight should make a clay body usable for a monumental piece, with walls inches thick. Because these expanded products are so coarse, a smooth clay surface is obtained only by working on it with a flexible metal rib. These fluffy pieces burn out in the firing and the shrinkage of the clay during firing tends to compress and diminish the air pockets left by these materials.

Fiberglass cloth can also be embedded in wet clay to give it tremendous tensile strength. In fact, any fiber can be used to help increase the tensile strength of a body, making it more flexible to work with in the plastic state. An addition of 0.5 to 1 percent of *fiberglass strands* to the clay body will produce a very strong and malleable clay body. *Nylon fiber*, again used at 0.5 to 1 percent of the total dry body weight, will provide the same flexibility in the plastic state. I suggest using these additions of nylon and fiberglass only for handbuilding—not for throwing on the wheel—unless you wear surgical gloves, since the fibers can really irritate your skin.

Colorants

Colorants are metallic oxides used to alter the fired color of a clay body. They include such common metallic oxides as iron, manganese, cobalt, and copper, as well as commercially prepared stains.

Iron oxide is the principal colorant used in low-fire clay bodies. You can vary the color of a light- or white-burning clay body by adding 1 to 5 percent iron oxide for a light buff, or 5 to 15 percent for a brown to dark red. But remember you'll be fluxing the clay as you color it. It is also much cheaper to find a low-fire red clay to use in your formula than to add pure iron oxide.

Commercially prepared stains offer a wider and subtler range of colors than do the metallic oxides. Stains contain oxides, either singly or in combination, which have been fritted with flux and clay.

When making colorant additions to a clay body, it is very important to mix them thoroughly in the dry state, as any accumulated stain or oxide could cause a swelling or blistering in the clay wall, called *bloating*.

Colored clays can be swirled or marbled into a white clay body. Definite patterns can be built up with differently colored clay bodies, so that glazing is often unnecessary or can be kept to a minimum. (See photoessay on Richard Shaw, page 40.)

Here are a few examples of clay body colors obtainable by adding oxides or stains. The percentage given is the proportion of colorant in the total dry weight of the clay body. Most commercial stains are required in amounts of 5 to 15 percent. Obviously these will work better in a white- or light-firing body.

Blue:	0.5 to 1.5 percent cobalt oxide or cobalt carbonate.
Green:	0.5 to 1 percent chrome oxide.
Brown:	3 to 5 percent iron oxide.
Dark Red:	10 to 15 percent iron oxide.
Yellow:	8 percent commercial yellow stain.

Putting It All Together

Before we run off and start making pieces, let's look at a few phenomena closely related to the materials we choose to make them with. In order to get a working clay we need to add enough water to our dry ingredients to make them plastic. This is called the *water of plasticity*. Our goal is to change wet plastic shapes into hard permanent objects. This entails drying and firing.

Drying and Green Strength

The water used to hold a clay body together for forming will evaporate when the piece is left to dry. When this happens the particles of the clay body move closer together, taking up the space left by the water. This causes shrinkage of the entire piece. Very fine-grained materials—that is, the more plastic ones, such as ball clay and bentonite—will shrink more than coarser materials, because there are more spaces between the particles filled with water. If there is a great loss of water, or water is lost too rapidly, cracking will result.

The more plastic the material is, the more it will shrink. The more it shrinks, the greater its tendency to crack. At the same time, the more it shrinks, the stronger the clay becomes when it is fully dried. When clay pieces are fully air-dried but not yet fired, they are termed *green*. *Green strength* is important in handling unfired pieces—carrying them and loading them in the kiln. Green strength is also related to the method of forming. The more compression exerted on the clay particles during forming, the higher its green strength. It is highest for extruded bodies, less for pieces made on the wheel, and least for slipcast ware.

Some Good Preventive Medicine

Dry your pieces as slowly as possible, keeping them out of the sun and drafts. A *damp closet* is ideal for drying things slowly. This is an area where high humidity can be maintained. If a closet isn't available, merely close off some shelving with thin plastic, allowing a flap door for getting in and out. Put buckets of water inside your damp closet to increase the moisture. If you are only working on one or two pieces at a time, it's more convenient to keep them covered individually in thin plastic. They can also be moistened by light spraying with water from a plant mister to keep surfaces, especially thin edges, as moist as their interiors.

Dry your pieces as evenly as possible, turning them over from time to time when practical. Or dry them on a rack that allows

air to circulate around the bottoms of the pieces.

If cracking and warping persist, *open up* your clay body. That is, make additions of larger particled material, such as grog or silica, that will help your clay body dry without too much shrinking and cracking.

Firing and the Dreaded Quartz Inversion

Before loading anything in the kiln, you should make sure your *greenware* is very dry. When possible I press the bottom of a piece to my cheek to check its coolness. The bottom is usually the last place to dry, and coolness indicates moisture. Leave those cool-bottomed pieces to dry before loading them in a kiln.

Greenware must be fired very slowly in the initial stages, as there is still some water of plasticity that needs to be driven off. Rapid initial firing could cause steam to form inside your piece, which might cause it to explode. Then there is the *chemically combined water* (recall the kaolinite formula), which must be vaporized. At about 600°C all the water in the clay body is gone. Any organic matter in the clay is also oxidized and vaporized in these early stages of firing.

During the heating process, more shrinkage of the clay body occurs. As indicated in the "Flux" section, most materials will shrink upon heating, and each material has a certain rate at which it does so, shown by its coefficient of expansion. Using fluxes with low coefficients can decrease the amount of shrinkage during firing.

All clays contain some free silica in the form of quartz crystals. We may even add some silica (or *flint* as it is often called) to a clay body to help with glaze fit (see chapter 4). Quartz undergoes a change in its crystal arrangement when it reaches 573°C. The crystals that normally exist below 573°C are known as *alpha quartz* and the first form they change to above 573°C is known as *beta quartz*. This change, from alpha to beta quartz, is accompanied by an increase in volume of about 2 percent. The reaction is reversible, so that on cooling there is a 2 percent decrease in volume going from beta to alpha quartz. The consequent expansion and contraction during firing and cooling exert tremendous force on the clay body and should therefore be passed through very slowly. Diminishing the amount of free quartz in a clay body will diminish the risk of cracking due to quartz inversion. When pieces crack during the cooling period it is known as *dunting*. Dunting cracks have sharp smooth edges, since they occur after the body has matured and vitrified. So do not be tempted to cool a kiln too quickly either. Quartz inversion is the deadliest gun in town.

Shrinkage: The Test

How much a clay body shrinks when fired depends on the materials put into it and the temperature to which it's fired.

Most low-fire bodies can keep their total fired shrinkage—from plastic state to fired state—below 10 percent, but again practical considerations must prevail. The clay body that works in every way you ask it to, but shrinks 15 percent without warping or cracking your pieces, is successful.

Shrinkage tests, as well as with the absorption and slump tests that follow, should be done for all clay bodies.

1. Make several bars at least 12 centimeters long and 1 centimeter thick from the wet clay of the consistency you plan to use.

2. Scratch two marks on each bar, exactly 100 millimeters (10 centimeters) apart.

3. Dry the bars completely.

4. Measure the distance between the two marks. Each millimeter is 1 percent of the total. If the distance now measures 97 millimeters after drying, then drying shrinkage was 3 percent.

5. Fire the bars to whatever temperature you are testing them at; when cool, mea-

sure the distance again. If it now measures 95 millimeters, the firing shrinkage was 2 percent and the total shrinkage 5 percent.

Absorption

During firing, as a clay body approaches its maturation point, the particles pull together tighter and tighter, giving the fired body its strength. To indicate how "tight" a clay body gets, we use an *absorption test* to see how much water it can still absorb after it's fired. Some clay bodies will never reach zero absorption, but in general the higher they are fired toward their maturation point, the closer they approach an absorption of zero, and the stronger they become.

1. Weigh a fired sample of clay on a gram scale.

2. Place the sample in a container of boiling water and let it boil for at least two hours.

3. Take the sample out, wipe off the water on the surface, and weigh again.

4. The percent absorption is equal to

$$\frac{\text{final weight after boiling} - \text{original weight before boiling}}{\text{original weight before boiling}} \times 100$$

There is no reason why absorption greater than 10 percent should be tolerated. Such a body will be very weak and fragile. Even at 10 percent the clay body is open and porous enough to be used as ovenware, able to accommodate itself to the contraction and expansion brought about by cooking. But it's possible to use fluxes with a low coefficient of expansion to reduce the absorption of a clay body and make it stronger and less susceptible to thermal shock.

If you were testing a clay body at cone 05 and it had a high absorption, the next step would be to fire it to a higher temperature. For example, the standard clay body of 60 percent ball clay and 40 percent talc has an absorption of 14 percent when fired to cone 05. Firing it to cone 1 diminishes that to 9.5 percent.

From Start to Slump

Testing a new clay body to find its optimum firing range requires patient step-by-step firings. Start at, say, cone 05, doing shrinkage and absorption tests, and proceed to the higher temperatures. When the absorption starts to decrease substantially, a *slump test* is in order. This simply entails placing a sample bar of a test clay between two supports at the ends (kiln shelf posts laid on their sides work well for this) so that the bar is unsupported in the middle. A clay bar made for shrinkage testing will serve for the slump test. If the bar distorts, or slumps, bending downward, you know the last firing was too hot for that clay body. Some clay bodies will gradually approach this slumping temperature, while others will jump to it like there was no tomorrow.

Thermal Shock: After the Fire

If any of the fired ware is to be used for cooking or baking, or even to hold hot coffee or tea, then a *thermal-shock test* should be done. The test pieces should be the same shape and covered with the same glaze or glazes you intend to use on your final pieces, as both shape and glaze fit play important parts in resistance to thermal shock. Large flat shapes, such as plates and platters, tend to crack upon heating more frequently than any other shape. Up to a point, thinner-walled pieces are less susceptible to thermal-shock cracks than other pieces, since shock is partially dependent on the temperature differences between the inner and outer faces of a fired piece of clay—the thinner the walls, the less temperature difference.

There are two approaches to shock testing. The first is to simply test several samples

as you intend to use them—for example, by pouring boiling coffee into a mug. The second is to *severely* test the samples—by putting the test pieces in a freezer for several hours, taking them out, and immediately pouring boiling water into them or placing them in a preheated oven. The results can be shattering. The point is, if your ware can pass the severe test, you need never worry about thermal shocking. On the other hand, they should never receive such severe treatment in daily use, so that the first test may be all that is necessary.

Perfect Bodies

As you may suspect by now, there is no such thing as "the perfect clay body." Formulation of clay bodies is always a matter of balance—having to open a fantastically plastic body or plasticize a minimally shrinking short body—in order to achieve good fired results.

Bodies for most plastic work—throwing, jiggering, handbuilding—require 60 to 70 percent clay. The other 30 or 40 percent is used to mature the clay at a low temperature. If you don't care about fired strength and would rather have less shrinkage, then you can use the ball-clay-talc body or some other combination that will give you those results.

Even if you're going to buy a clay body whose ingredients you don't know, it's wise to refer to those materials and tests which are available. These will help you to better understand the process of working with clay and make it easier to find a suitable replacement, should that become necessary. After all, you may outgrow your clay body. Your supplier may quit on you. Or the clay you've grown accustomed to may start to give you problems.

White Bodies

Since there are no naturally occurring low-fire white clays, a white low-fire clay body must always start with a very refractory material.

Only the presence of iron oxide and other minerals in common red clays makes them mature at low temperatures. For whiteware, then, we must balance the use of a highly refractory material with nonplastic fluxes.

Most commercial low-fire white bodies are fluxed with talc as a major ingredient. Talc is safe (in a wet, mixed state) and inexpensive, has a long firing range, and maintains the whiteness of the clay. The standard formula—60 percent ball clay, 40 percent talc—is usually sold as cone 05 clay. As mentioned, this body is weak and porous, having an absorption of 14 percent at cone 05. Merely firing to cone 1 will decrease its absorption to 9.5 percent and help tighten it.

Here, then, are some of the formulas I've tested.

Ball Clay 60%; Talc 40%:

    drying shrinkage: 3%

    total shrinkage at cone 05: 4%

    absorption at cone 05: 14.5%

    total shrinkage at cone 1: 6%

    absorption at cone 1: 9.5%

    fired color: white

Ball Clay 50%; EPK 20%; Talc 25%; Nepheline Syenite 5%:

    drying shrinkage: 4%

    total shrinkage at cone 05: 5%

    absorption at cone 05: 17%

    total shrinkage at cone 1: 10%

    absorption at cone 1: 6.5%

    fired color: white

Ball Clay 35%; EPK 35%; Frit 54 20%; Kingman Feldspar 10%:

    drying shrinkage: 5%

    total shrinkage at cone 05: 12%

    absorption at cone 05: 4.5%

    total shrinkage at cone 1: 14%

    absorption at cone 1: 1%

    fired color: white

Ball Clay 18%; EPK 27%; Silica 5%; Lepidolite 15%; Talc 5%; Nepheline Syenite 30%:

    drying shrinkage: 4%

    total shrinkage at cone 05: 8%

    absorption at cone 05: 9%

    total shrinkage at cone 1: 12%

    absorption at cone 1: 0.5%

    fired color: white

Ball Clay 60%; Talc 10%; Pyrophyllite 20%; Frit 54 10%:

    drying shrinkage: 4%

    total shrinkage at cone 05: 8%

    absorption at cone 05: 7.5%

    fired color: white

Ball Clay 60%; Frit 54 20%; Wollastonite 20%:

    drying shrinkage: 5%

    total shrinkage at cone 05: 9.5%

    absorption at cone 05: 0.5%

    fired color: beige

Ball Clay 35%; EPK 20%; Talc 15%; Nepheline Syenite 10%; Frit 3191 20%:

    drying shrinkage: 5%

    total shrinkage at cone 05: 9.5%

    absorption at cone 05: 1%

    fired color: cream

Remember, you can increase the plasticity of any clay by adding up to 2 percent bentonite (by weight); for better drying, with less warping and cracking, you can add up to 20 percent grog or sand. For tensile strength during shaping, 1 percent nylon or fiberglass shreds can be added. The usefulness of nylon and fiberglass was discovered as a result of artistic experiment, and the materials' primary use remains in that realm, so commercial clay manufacturers do not yet offer these reinforcing fillers in their clay bodies. If you want them, you'll have to put them in yourself or order your clay specially made.

Red Earthenware Bodies

In formulating red earthenware bodies, there is more freedom in the choice of materials, since whiteness is no longer an objective. For these bodies it is always more economical and practical to rely on a local red clay or even a local fire clay. Because of this, it is difficult and certainly frustrating to print clay-body recipes using materials unobtainable by so many readers. If you've understood the principles behind clay bodies, you should have no trouble creating an earthenware body. You can, in fact, take the recipes for low-fire white bodies and substitute fire clays for some or all of the ball clay and EPK.

So a low-fire red body might look like this:

Fire clay	65%
Local Red Clay	10%
Talc	25%

Keeping It Together

For all our scientific knowledge and theorizing, we can never be absolutely sure about our clays and glazes until they're given back to us from the kiln. Once you've agonized over your materials, and your clay body is formulated, it's time to turn your work area into a laboratory and do some testing. Since formulation is largely a theoretical step, it helps to mix a small batch of your formula to test its working and firing characteristics before committing yourself to expending the time, energy, and money to mix a large batch. If you are doing small to medium-sized work, 25 pounds ought to go a long way. If you're a monumental achiever, it's still well to limit your test batches to 25 pounds because of the potential for disappointment. Don't spend a week working on one piece with a new clay body! This warning applies equally to clay you buy from a supplier: try out 25 or 50 pounds of it first, before committing yourself to larger amounts. Simulate some of the more difficult situations you might put your clay through. Join pieces of clay (appendages, handles, etc.) together and watch for cracking in the firing. If you throw, throw a wide thin bowl and see how much it warps while drying and after firing.

Mixing a test batch requires weighing dry ingredients. A 25-pound kitchen scale is ideal for this purpose, and it will be put to lots of other uses in your studio. Also, if you haven't already got a notebook in your lab, get one. Keep track of everything you do, so that when you mix the "perfect clay" you won't have to wonder how it came about.

Another essential for mixing dry ingredients is a dust respirator, available at hardware stores and ceramic-supply stores. Wear it. It will save your mucous membranes and lungs for better things. It is impossible to mix dry ingredients, regardless of how careful you are, without generating fine dust. Some materials, like a few California talcs, contain asbestos, and are doubly noxious.

As you mix your dry ingredients, be careful not to drop them from great heights. Instead, gently ease them into containers, to keep the dust down. If you have a container with a tight-fitting lid, you can dry-mix all your ingredients by shaking it, or by rolling it back and forth. Otherwise, mix by hand as best you can. A large wire whisk is good for dry mixing and creates very little dust. Dry mixing is important, for it disperses all the ingredients evenly.

Then—just add water. It generally takes

about 25 percent water by weight to get a clay to a workable consistency. Since water weighs 8 pounds per gallon, you'll add about ¾ gallon of water to 25 pounds of dry ingredients. Keep track of the amounts you add in your clay-test notebook!

Mix the clay by hand until it's fairly homogeneous. Then break it into thirds or quarters and *wedge* it—that is, knead it without getting any additional air into it— until the clay has no air pockets left. When mixing by hand, it's easiest to mix the clay with an excess of water and let it dry out to a workable consistency.

Wrap your wedged clay in plastic to keep it from drying. Let at least one of the clay balls you've wedged sit in its plastic wrapper for a week or more, as aging helps to plasticize the clay. Save a few pounds for shrinkage, absorption, and slump tests and use the rest any way you like.

The only way to determine the clay's qualities in the wet state is to use the clay. For the beginning student, it is very difficult to determine the limits of a clay body. Any clay body may have the capacity to do far more than you are capable of asking it to do.

But if it won't respond to what you *do* do to it, then it may need to be changed.

Most beginning pottery students doing wheel work blame themselves for unsuccessful attempts because they haven't the criteria or experience with which to judge their clay. I've seen some of them, however, try to throw with clay that was so wet it was oozing, after having thrown the same piece of clay dozens of times. (One of the results of repeated throwing with lots of water is the removal of the more plastic particles from the clay. The plastic material is finer-grained than the rest and is easily removed by the action of the water used for lubrication and by the friction of hands while throwing.)

You will develop a sense about the clay you use as you go along: not just how wet or dry it ought to be for any particular operation, but how plastic or grogged. It is very instructive to see what other people can do with the same clay body you're using. If you use a commercially prepared clay, the manufacturer is likely to have some fired pieces he keeps for display. They are usually pretty uninspiring, but ask some of the local people using his clay and pay them a visit.

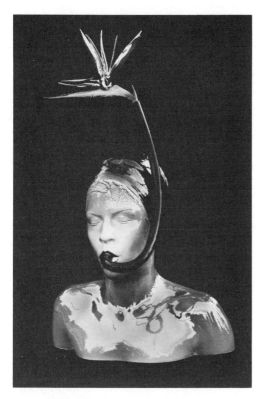

by Will Herrera

Will Herrera has supported himself for many years by producing ceramic pins. Most of the pins he makes now are simple shapes with decals fired onto them; he designs the decals and has them made by a ceramic-decal company. He also manufactures slipcast leg and foot planters (see Plate 9) and cast clocks. He likes slipcasting because of the clean lines and surfaces possible. When doing his limited production, slipcasting helps him produce forms quickly, enabling him to spend more time decorating and glazing.

"The Bird of Paradise"

It was a late Friday night when Herrera and two friends showed up at my studio. Leonard would assist him and Janet would serve as the model for the plaster mold. That same night Herrera and Leonard constructed the wood frame that would be the back retaining wall for the plaster and limit the mold to Janet's head and shoulders. Herrera traced onto plywood the contour of Janet's body where he wanted the mold to end—one piece for the front contour and one for the back, so the two would come together just below Janet's shoulders. The plywood was cut with a jigsaw and holes were drilled so the pieces could be bolted to 2-by-4-inch supports.

The next morning, Herrera went down to the beach near my studio and dug up about a hundred pounds of wet river sand. This was to be used instead of clay to establish the parting line on Janet for a two-piece mold. His idea for the project at this time was to have the cast bust with a bird-of-paradise flower growing from the head. He later decided to add a snorkel from which the flower grew.

The front part of Janet's head and shoulders was to be cast first. It took Herrera about an hour to position her face up on the concrete floor, lying in the back contour frame and having the front frame attached so it didn't pinch her too much.

When he was satisfied it would work, she was prepared for casting. She put on a bathing cap and plugged her nostrils with tissue so plaster wouldn't run up her nose. Herrera covered her face and shoulders with mineral oil, which served as a sizing compound. A minimum amount of oil was used so it wouldn't clog the pores of the plaster after it hardened. A snorkel would serve as Janet's connection to air while she was covered with plaster.

Let me say here that if you want to make a face mold, find a model who trusts you and won't panic while the plaster is drying. Being pinned under plaster is not something I would readily volunteer for, so I was fairly impressed by this woman's calmness and trust. She lay down and rested her head on a small towel used as a pillow. Almost like shoulder stocks, the wooden frames were bolted into place. The wet sand was packed down all around her head and shoulders and built up to an even level that divided her into top and bottom halves. Keys were gouged out of the wet sand with a spoon.

Herrera and Leonard then mixed the plaster. Each had a 5-gallon plastic bucket about ¾ full of water. They sifted plaster into the water until it was saturated and a little mound of plaster remained above the waterline. They let the plaster slake for two minutes and then each mixed his bucket of plaster by hand. Rapidly, Herrera checked Janet's snorkel to make sure she could get air, she closed her eyes, and they

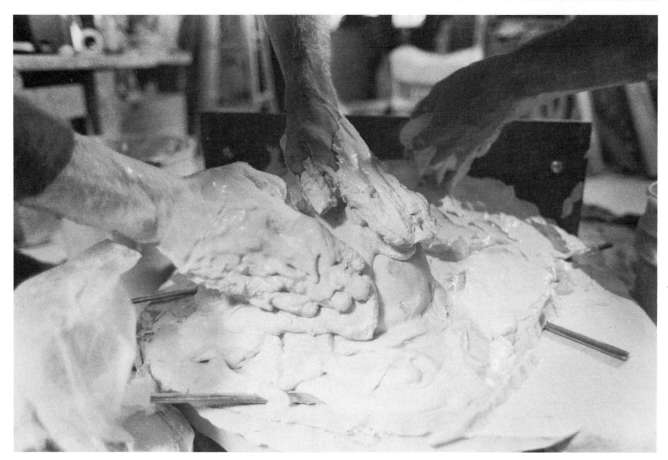

heaped plaster onto her. In order to keep the mold light and limit the amount of plaster used, Herrera did not pour the plaster all the way to the top and side retaining walls. Instead he scooped the plaster out by hand and mounded it so the plaster walls were at least 2 inches thick all the way around. Janet was still and limp. Within five minutes of the initial heaping, the plaster began to harden and get warm. After ten minutes, Herrera pulled the mold and snorkel away from her head and she still looked calm and peaceful.

After a short break, Herrera sized the first piece of the mold and positioned it on the floor. Janet then lay down with her face in the mold; she could breathe through the hole left by the snorkel. The frames were again bolted into place. Herrera placed about six knives around the perimeter of the first piece—a safety precaution in case the two pieces of plaster didn't separate as they were supposed to. More plaster

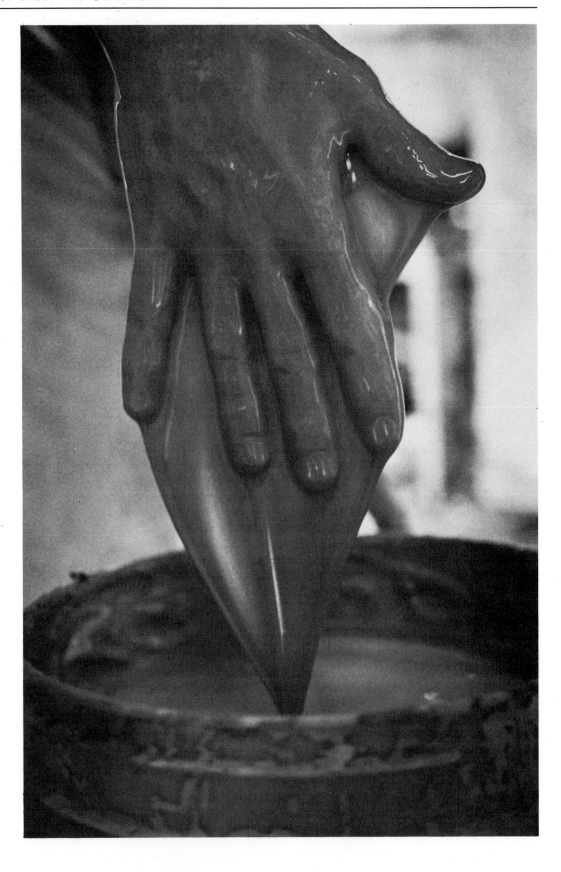

was mixed and shoveled onto the first mold piece and Janet. It took another ten minutes before the plaster hardened and the top mold piece was pulled away. The mold looked great, Janet had survived, and Herrera left for Los Angeles to get some work done.

Two weeks later David Powers and I flew to Los Angeles to see Herrera finish the piece in his small 12-by-20-foot studio crammed with glazes, glaze tests, and odds and ends of some of his work.

The mold had had two weeks to dry and was ready for casting. Normally it takes three or four castings before a good cast is achieved, but this mold gave a perfect cast the first time Herrera used it, on a trial run just before we got there.

The mold was first cleaned with a damp sponge to remove any clay particles from the last casting that could cause tiny bubbles in the next one. Then the two parts of the mold were tied together with several mold straps.

Since Herrera did not pour the plaster all the way to the retaining wall around the entire model when the mold was made, the end of the mold that needs to be sitting on the ground wasn't flat enough to do so without some help. So with the head end down and the shoulder end up, the mold was propped up by bags of plastic clay and cinder blocks. Also, since the mold is so large that it requires a lot of slip to fill it, it would be too heavy to lift to pour out the excess slip. So Herrera inserted a short section of plastic tubing in the hole left by the snorkel to function as a drain, and used a plastic bottle cap to stopper it while the clay was setting up in the mold.

A retaining wall of plastic clay was built around the base of the mold to serve as a *reservoir* so slip could be poured above the base of the mold and allowed to settle down to it.

Herrera uses a commercially prepared slip clay body he mixes in his homemade blunger, 50 pounds at a time. He hand-mixes every batch just before using it to test its deflocculation—the slip should "web" between the fingers, and when squeezed in the hand it should leave a crisp imprint.

Herrera poured the slip steadily into the middle of the mold until it filled the reservoir space, then let it stand for an hour in the mold, until the walls were thick enough (about ¼ inch). He pulled the bottle cap off the drain and let the slip drain out, then lifted the mold to pour the final excess out the base.

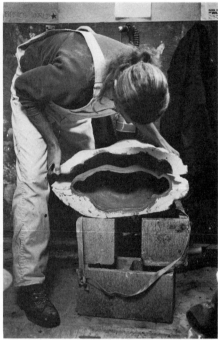

About five hours later, Herrera trimmed the bottom and added a coil of clay to the inside edge of the bottom to give the base better support. Another five hours passed before the cast was dry enough to be removed from the mold. The fresh casting was covered with plastic to keep it moist while the other sections planned for the piece were cast.

Herrera next cast a snorkel in the snorkel mold he had made some time before for another piece. When slip is poured into a mold it needs to displace the air already in the mold. Some shapes, like the J-shape of the snorkel, make this difficult and cause enough suction during the casting that the sides of the cast will slump inward when pulled from the mold. Drilling a hole toward the bottom of the mold and placing a nail in it before casting will prevent that suction. The snorkel cast up in about an hour and was removed from the mold and placed under plastic.

The final component for this piece was to be a cast of a bird-of-paradise flower. So we walked over to an obliging neighbor's backyard and Herrera picked the best of the lot.

It took almost a full day to make this mold. Though it was much smaller than the bust, the flower presented a number of problems, since the petals were too soft to cast—they would just float in the plaster in their natural state—and they jutted out into three or four different planes. But, if the flower were flattened, it would certainly detract from the reality of the object Herrera was trying to capture. However, he had it all under control.

To solve the problem of softness, he brushed the flower with melted sculpture wax. A thin layer of wax gives enough support to the fragile petals to allow them to be cast. The wax must be kept thin so the detail of the petals isn't lost.

The fairly rigid flower was then laid flat on a slab of plastic clay, with one set of petals in the plane of the clay slab. What Herrera and

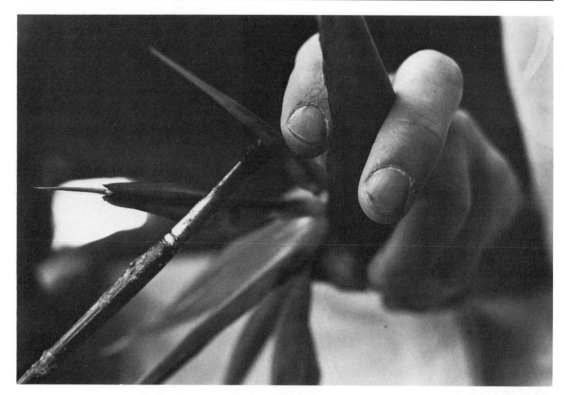

Nature had done was to pair the petals off. Just because they grew away from each other didn't mean they couldn't be pressed together for the purpose of making a mold. So the petals were paired off and laid flat. However, a strip of plastic clay was wedged in between the petal pairs so that the mold would be made as if the petals were one piece. A cast taken of this mold, though, would give him enough room to cut the petals apart and bend them back into their original position. This was an impressive solution to the casting of a fragile object. It also meant that Herrera spent as much time cutting, cleaning, and positioning the casting as he would have if he had done the flower by hand.

After the first half of the mold was made, Herrera not only made keys in the plaster but also scraped thin channels from the ends of the petals to the edges of the mold. These *bleeder lines* insure that no air gets trapped in these thin sections of the flower. Instead of creating an air bubble in the wall of the casting, the air gets pushed out the bleeder line.

The slip for casting the bird of paradise was thinned with water and cast very thin, about $\frac{1}{8}$ inch. This was to decrease its weight so it wouldn't put too much pressure on the snorkel on which it would rest. This excess water caused an abnormal amount of *flanging*—that is, slip that gets between the walls of the two pieces of the mold. It meant a little more cleanup but afforded the thinness Herrera was after.

Before assembling the pieces, Herrera cleaned all three casts using a fettling knife to scrape the seam lines at a diagonal, and then sponging them smooth.

The snorkel was scored and slipped at the mouthpiece and inserted into the scored and slipped mouth of the bust. The snorkel casting was still wet enough so Herrera could bend it toward the bust and attach a spot on the straight tube section to a small area on the bathing cap, giving it some needed support. These two pieces were then allowed to dry for a day until they were firm enough to support the bird-of-paradise casting.

The end of the stem of the flower was scored and slipped and stuck down the snorkel top about 2 inches. Herrera then built up clay from the worktable to support the overhanging flower while it dried. (If he hadn't cast the flower so thin, I don't think he could have gotten away with attaching and firing it as part of the piece. He would have had to fire it separately and attach it afterward with epoxy.)

Herrera used commercial underglazes, glazes, lusters, and decals to finish the piece. The flower was airbrushed with opaque mauve, blue, and orange underglaze, while the bathing cap band was underglazed in mauve. A white opaque satin glaze was poured and brushed over the en-

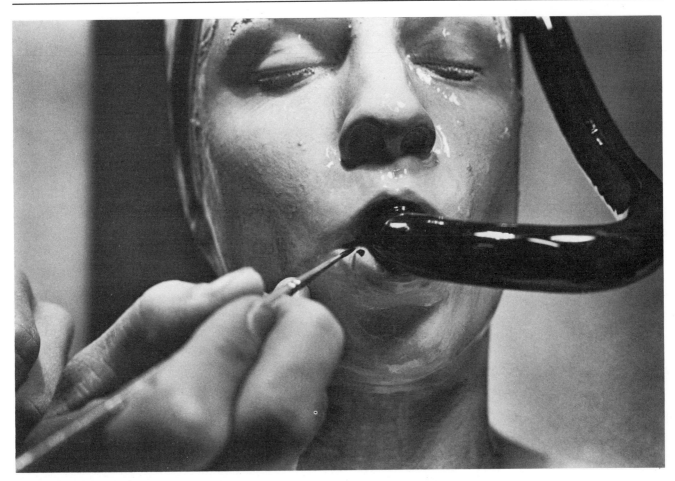

tire piece except the snorkel and bathing cap. A blue glaze was then
airbrushed lightly over the white on the bust, leaving only a small area
around the nose and mouth white. The snorkel was brushed with a deep
luminous blue glaze and the bathing cap with a deep glossy green. The
piece was then fired to cone 06 to mature all the glazes. Next he used a
small commercial flower decal repeatedly on the bathing cap. The piece
was then refired to cone 018 to fire the decals on. It looked very good,
but Herrera wanted a little more flash. So he used platinum luster on
the lips (this he did more to cover up some blue glaze that had run unevenly onto them than because he really wanted to luster the lips) and
airbrushed platinum luster on the shoulders and back of the bust and on
some of the flower petals. A cone 019 firing, and out came "The Bird of
Paradise" seen in color in Plate 8.

Central Casting

The discovery that clay could be made into liquid slip and poured into plaster molds must have shot the heartbeats of the captains of the ceramic industry off their charts. It was a great technical blessing for commercial ceramics, which facilitated the easy reproduction of any particular product, so that, literally, they could "make a million of 'em."

For the studio ceramicist, casting in plaster molds is a useful method of working for reasons other than mass production. *Slipcasting*, as the process is called, can produce difficult shapes unattainable by other means, particularly those representing "ceramics vérité," the reproduction of found objects. Casting can also insure a very smooth and slick surface, so important if the nature of the glazing demands no interference or competition. In general, the studio person uses cast shapes as starting points, rather than ends in themselves. Shapes that can be altered, textured, or added to, help expedite the forming process while allowing each piece to retain its uniqueness. Some artists will do a series of pieces with shapes made from molds and then throw the molds away, much as a printmaker would destroy a plate after printing an edition. Will Herrera (see preceding photoessay, page 15) has even broken some of his molds, cast the resulting bits and pieces, and assembled them into new forms.

In large factories, the mold maker is one of the most important cogs in the operation. The molds get constant use and need to be replaced often with no perceptible change from the originals. On a commercial level, casting is an exacting and precise method of working. Studio people do not need to work with the same precision; indeed, laxness is often what allows cast work to gain character and not look like a hundred other pieces.

You should have access to all the means of commercial ceramics and be able to use them to your own ends. If you find that the *process* of slipcasting changes your work to something you're not happy with, then don't use it.

Slipcasting

A casting body is a clay body formulated to be made into a liquid state (known as *casting slip*) so that it can be poured into plaster molds. Casting slips take advantage of the chemical properties of clay to get a homogeneous, dense, liquid form.

Flocculation and Deflocculation

There were no special conditions under which we produced bodies in chapter 1. We used clay as it came from the ground or bag, properly milled and screened. By adding enough water, workable plastic clay was produced. No electrodes had to be implanted or any dark incantations recited. Yet clay consists of large particles clustering or *floccing* together due to attracting electrical charges. If water is added to a normally wetted clay body and then mixed in a container until a liquid slip is formed, the clay will soon settle to the bottom. Where one heavier-than-water clay particle goes, the rest will follow in the normal *flocculated* state. Originally, this was how slipcasting was done. But the settling of the clay was only one problem. The other was that to turn clay into slip required enormous amounts of water. This caused the plaster molds to get very wet very quickly and thus lose the capacity to absorb enough water to produce a good casting.

It was later discovered that certain chemicals, when added to clay slip, will *disperse* the clay throughout the slip, and prevent it from settling. This makes sense now that we know about the chemical and electrical nature of clay. The chemicals change the electrical charges on the particles of clay so that they are the same, and therefore repel each other. This condition is known as *deflocculation*.

Flocculated clay particles act like cattle corralled in a tight pen, forced to remain in close contact. Deflocculated clay particles get a bigger pen, and act as if there were rigid horizontal poles connecting all the cattle so they can't get any closer to each other.

One of the consequences of floccing clay particles is that they trap films of water inside themselves. (Again, imagine that there are unbreakable—inescapable—balloons underfoot all the tightly penned cattle.) When the group is dispersed, i.e. deflocculated, this trapped water is released into the slip (as if the balloons were released to float among the cattle). This process provides a casting slip that contains no more than 2 percent more water than an ordinary plastic clay body. Whereas it might take 50 or 60 percent water to make a flocculated clay slip of the right consistency for casting, only 25 to 35 percent water is necessary to make a deflocculated slip of the same consistency. This creates a high *bulk density*—more clay per volume of slip, or less water in the slip. Plaster molds will not clog as easily and thicker pieces can be cast.

Deflocculants

The chemicals added to a clay-and-water mixture to disperse the clay particles throughout the mixture are called *deflocculants*.

The standard deflocculants are *sodium carbonate*, usually referred to as *soda ash*, and *sodium silicate*, also known as *water glass*. There are other materials that will deflocculate clay, but these two work well for most situations, which is why they are readily available and widely used. They generally produce better results when used together.

Sodium carbonate, Na_2CO_3, is a white crystalline powder. When used alone it produces flabby, weak casts that will not hold together in the mold. It also has a short *fluidity range*; that is, the range within which it will deflocculate a clay slip is relatively narrow. Since too little deflocculant won't deflocculate and too much will *reflocculate* the slip, it is desirable to have a wide range within which to work.

You do get a wide range with sodium silicate, $Na_2O \cdot nSiO_2$, where *n* is a variable from 1.6 to 3.75. You should always know which type of sodium silicate you are using in order to repeat your results. Sodium silicate is always sold in liquid form. When used alone, the resulting casts are usually brittle and difficult to work with.

Some other deflocculants include sodium tannate, sodium pyrophosphate, and sodium hydroxide, which is very caustic and must be handled carefully.

Defloccing Together

When used together in the right ratio, soda ash and sodium silicate will eliminate each other's faults. Finding the right ratio is a trial-and-error process. In general, clay bodies of low plasticity or with low ball-clay content need more sodium silicate than soda ash, since the organic matter in ball clays helps stabilize deflocculated slip and the same effect can be reproduced with sodium silicate. This situation might require the chemicals in the ratio of 3 sodium silicate to 1 soda ash. If the opposite is true—i.e., there is plenty of ball clay—the ratio might be reversed.

One should always use less than 1 percent total deflocculant by weight in relation to the dry ingredients of the clay body, as an excess will slowly seal the pores of plaster molds with an insoluble film of calcium silicate, making it almost impossible to remove a casting from it.

All of the principles of formulating clay learned in chapter 1 are applicable to slipcasting bodies. The key again is balance. For example, a slip that has too many fine particles—that is, is excessively plastic—not only runs the risk of the shrink-warp-crack syndrome, but will cast up very slowly and be difficult to release from the mold. On the other hand, too coarse a slip will be difficult to deflocculate.

Less plastic material is needed for slipcasting than for a normal clay body used for throwing or handbuilding. Fifty percent plastic material is sufficient to keep good green strength and facilitate trimming. If you are aiming to get a super-tight casting body, one that may even be translucent, you can get the plastic clay level down to 35 percent and use 65 percent flux. Such a body, however, is often difficult to deflocculate.

Clays with a lot of iron oxide are also difficult to deflocculate. If you want to try slipcasting with a red clay body, it is better to use a dark fire clay or local red clay, rather than adding iron oxide to a white-body formula. Clay grogs, however, *can* be used in casting bodies with no problems; they will remain suspended without sinking to the bottom of the slip barrel. In general, high *alkalinity* (chemically basic as opposed to acidic) will cause or tend to cause deflocculation in a clay slip, so that feldspars and nepheline syenite might be helpful in a clay body that needed deflocculating.

Problems, Problems

If you cannot deflocculate a slip, it might be caused by the presence of sulphate, calcium, magnesium, iron, or aluminum salts in the materials or, more likely, the water. These are all flocculants. Adding some barium carbonate, $BaCO_3$—from 0.02 to 0.1 percent of the weight of the dry clay materials—should help restore the balance in favor of deflocculation.

Some other common sources of these soluble salts are talc and frits. Don't panic. You need to be aware of where they are coming from, and you just learned how to deal with them should they interfere with your casting plans.

Another flocculant that should definitely be avoided in casting bodies is montmorillonite, the mineral substance of bentonite. This is a good time to think about the problem of combining a slipcast object with forms made with normally mixed clay. If you want to join the two together, it is advantageous, if not necessary, to have fairly similar formulas, so that the shrinkage rates will be close enough to prevent them from cracking apart. In this case then, you might want to avoid using bentonite in your normal body.

Plaster itself is a flocculant. That is in fact one of the reasons a plaster mold works so well. Clay at the surface of the mold not only has its water drawn out but is flocculated by the plaster. Here's the caution: if a cast just removed from the mold needs to be trimmed, it is best to throw that trimmed-off bit of clay away rather than recycle it back into slip. The plaster is somewhat soluble and can build up in the cast clay. The excess slip that is poured out of the mold while draincasting (see "Drain Molds," page 37) can be reused.

The addition of too much deflocculant to a casting slip will eventually thicken the slip as if it were flocculated. If it's a borderline case of overdeflocculation, you will have some problems with the casts sticking to the plaster molds, making removal difficult. There may also be some scumming on the ware and glaze crawling during the glaze firing.

Sometimes the surface of the slip will look like wet liver and have a jellylike texture. This is called *livering* and is caused by flocculation from excessive deflocculant or the presence of flocculating salts.

Tiny holes or *pinholes* on the casting are usually from air in the slip or mold. Hot or very dry plaster molds can also cause pinholing by sucking the water from the slip so quickly that air bubbles are formed in the slip.

Doing It

You can set up your "laboratory" for preparing and testing slipcasting bodies in much the same way you did in chapter 1, since you mix the dry ingredients of a slip clay body with the same methods and the same precautions (wear a dust respirator). Because the first thing you need to know about a slipcasting body is how well it will deflocculate, that is the first test to be done. Since this is a test just to determine the proper proportions of deflocculants, water, and clay body, it can be done with small amounts of materials. After determining these proportions, a larger test batch can be made for actual test castings.

It is efficient and easily calculable to do this test using metric measurements. This requires, then, a *gram scale* and some *graduated cylinders*, measuring at least 50 milliliters (that's 50 cubic centimeters). The gram scale is not a great expense. It will come in very handy for measuring out small glaze batches and tests, and it is needed for the clay-body absorption test.

This is a test to determine if a body will deflocculate with sodium silicate and sodium carbonate, and how much of the two used in equal amounts it takes to do the job. If the body you are testing is low or high in plastic material (refer back to page 29, "Defloccing Together"), you might want to skip ahead to the trial-and-error test.

1. Weigh out 1,000 grams of dry slip clay body.

2. Add 250 milliliters of water.

3. Mix the water and clay well and see what the consistency is like. If it's too dry and crumbly, keep adding carefully measured quantities of water until the clay is like slush. Remember that the deflocculated slip need not contain any more water than a normal plastic clay body, so you shouldn't add any more than 500 milliliters of water in all. You can readjust water in later tests if you like; that is, try to use less water later on for test-casting purposes, as an excess of water will cause

the casting to crack and/or stick to the molds. In order to recalculate for mixing larger batches in pounds, remember that 1 milliliter of water weighs 1 gram, so you've got the percentages all worked out for you. For example, if it takes 350 milliliters of water to get the clay body to slush, that's 35 percent water of the total dry weight of the 1,000-gram test batch.

4. Measure out 40 milliliters of hot water in a graduate. To that add 5 grams of sodium carbonate and 5 grams of liquid sodium silicate; then add enough hot water to bring the mixture up to 50 milliliters. You now have a solution with 10 percent of each of the deflocculants—for every 1 milliliter of water there is 0.10 gram of sodium carbonate and 0.10 gram of the liquid sodium silicate.

5. Add the deflocculant solution, a drop at a time, to the clay slush, stirring and mixing constantly. When and if the clay suddenly turns liquid, stop. Check the graduate and note how much solution you've used. Let the slip stand for at least an hour without stirring it to see whether it gels—that is, reverts to a thickened state. If it does, you've probably added too much deflocculant, or possibly not enough. Repeat the test and watch it closely.

Once you've determined the ratios of materials needed in your slip, you can mix up a bigger batch. There is a mixer, called a *blunger*, available commercially for mixing large batches of slip. This is merely a barrel with a motorized mixing blade. You can make your own by buying a long mixer attachment for an electric drill and finding your own barrel or container and securing the drill and mixer shaft inside the barrel so you don't have to hold it for two hours of mixing time.

Because a large batch contains much dry clay, it's easier to mix if you:

1. Measure out the amount of water needed for the batch and pour it into a large container.

2. Measure out the deflocculants needed and dissolve in hot water as shown in the last test. Add this to the water in container.

3. Mix up dry ingredients for slip clay body and add them to the water-deflocculant solution in container.

4. Mix for two hours. This mixing is called *blunging*.

Let the slip sit for a couple of days to age before you use it. Screen it through a 50-mesh screen before each use, getting all lumps out. Get all air bubbles out by pouring back and forth between containers and skimming bubbles off the top.

When pouring the slip into molds, pour a slow and steady stream. Try to pour gently into one corner of the mold, keeping air out. Don't shake or move the casting during or after pouring. If a casting is difficult to remove from a plaster mold, any of the following may be the reason:

1. There is too much plastic material in the slip body.

2. There is too much water in the slip body.

3. The mold is too wet.

One of the less scientific but more useful tests to determine whether a casting slip needs more deflocculant is to stir it with a glass rod. The groove left behind the rod should close immediately. The slip should also run off the rod and not adhere; the drops should be taken up immediately by the slip. For larger batches, stir the slip with your hand and see if it webs between your fingers. (See photo on page 18.) The ultimate test, of course, is to pour it in the molds and see if it works.

If nothing has happened with your test by the time you've used up all the deflocculant solution, repeat the test, but add 1 gram of *barium carbonate* to the 1,000 grams of dry clay body. If it still doesn't deflocculate, reread this chapter and check the ingredients in your slip clay body, changing any that have been listed as troublemakers.

If after rereading this chapter you determine that the ratio of deflocculants should be different, or if you want to try different ratios after testing some castings in plaster molds, you can repeat the testing procedures with this difference: measure the deflocculants into separate graduates. You can then try any combination of these two deflocculants, or any of the deflocculants listed, remembering not to add more than 10 grams total deflocculant to the 1,000-gram batch. The less deflocculant you have to use, the better your molds and castings will be.

Plaster: Good Impressions

Plaster is made from the mineral *gypsum*, which is in reality *calcium sulphate*. It is a dry white powder that is mixed with water. When wet, plaster replicates any form and surface it is poured over or into. After it dries it can remain porous enough to draw water from a plastic clay or a deflocculated clay slip, thus ensuring a known form and surface in clay within a reasonably short time.

Plaster comes in several forms, only two of which are important for clay work:

No. 1 Industrial Molding Plaster or *Pottery Plaster*, is the softest and most porous, also the least expensive and probably the most used. Good porosity in a mold is a necessity, especially when slip-casting, and the strength of molds made with pottery plaster are more than adequate.

No. 1 Casting Plaster has a small amount of hardening agent so it is slightly harder and less porous than pottery plaster. Molds made from casting plaster might last a little longer, but the casts made in them then take a little more time to set up.

Your plaster should be stored in as *dry* an atmosphere as possible, or it will absorb moisture from the air and get lumpy when you use it. Start with as fresh a batch as you can obtain, not with a bag that's been sitting around open.

A Plaster Place

Before bringing plaster into an area used for clay work, there are precautions you should take to prevent any plaster from getting into your clay or glazes. Particles of trapped gypsum can expand and pop big chunks of glaze off a piece months after it's been fired. It can also damage plumbing.

Using plaster requires a certain degree of good planning, since there is relatively little time between the mixing of plaster with water and its subsequent hardening. The mold you are making should be properly sized (see page 35) before mixing your plaster. Some means of cleaning up the mixing buckets and utensils needs to be close at hand. Keep a large (20- or 30-gallon) garbage can filled with water so that all the equipment can be dunked in the barrel, not rinsed in the sink where the plaster is flushed into the plumbing. Also have a bag or can available into which you can pour any excess plaster (and there should usually be some) and leave it to harden.

How Little Time You Have

The *setting time* is the time it takes for the plaster mixed with water to become hard. It is usually between ten and thirty minutes. After the plaster has lost its fluidity and has begun to thicken, you can carve it or move it around with your hands. This is called its *period of plasticity*, and lasts between five and ten minutes.

Mixing Plaster

Plaster for molds used for clay works best if:

1. The plaster is added *to* the water.

2. The plaster is sifted into the water gradually.

3. The plaster is used in a 3-to-2 proportion by *weight* to water—3 plaster, 2 water.

Plaster sets in direct proportion to the amount of plaster in the mix: the more plaster, the quicker it sets, the harder and less porous it becomes. Setting time is also shortened by agitating the mix more and by increasing the temperature of the water.

The ratio of plaster to water is important enough to require a scale to measure the two ingredients, ensuring that the resulting mold won't be weak and crumbly from too much water, or too hard and nonporous from too much plaster.

The first step is to determine *volume*—how much plaster is needed for what you are making. If you are good at estimating volumes, are usually able to say, "Say, that looks like a five-quart casserole to me," then this should be easy work. Just remember to overestimate so you won't have to quickly make up more plaster before the first pour hardens. *Plaster takes up about 35 percent of the volume in a plaster-water mixture of the consistency we want for clay work.* Water makes up 65 percent of the *volume* of the mixture then, right? So, determine the volume of wet plaster needed for casting and take 65 percent of that figure. Measure out that amount of water and weigh it. You now have the *weight* of the water. Simply multiply that number by $3/2$, remembering the 3-to-2 ratio, to determine the weight of plaster needed.

If an eyeball estimation of volume is difficult, then reduce forms to rectangular prisms and estimate by multiplying *length* by *width* by *height*. (V = L × W × H.)

Here are some other helpful figures:

1. There are 7.5 gallons of water in 1 cubic foot of water.

2. There are 231 cubic inches of water in 1 gallon of water.

3. One gallon of water weighs 8.3 pounds.

So, if you want to cast a simple plaster slab on which to dry clay or to carve for press molds, and you want the slab to be 20 inches long, 18 inches wide, and 3 inches thick, the volume would be 20 × 18 × 3, or 1,080 cubic inches. Water takes up 65 percent of this volume; or 1,080 × 0.65 equals 702 cubic inches. To get gallons, take 702 cubic inches divided by 231 cubic inches per gallon—just about 3 gallons of water. In weighing this out we find that 3 gallons of water weighs 25 pounds. Multiplying this by $3/2$ determines the weight of plaster, 37.5 pounds.

Ready to Pour

After you've determined the volume of water needed, poured it into a container and weighed it, and then determined the weight of plaster needed, you are ready to add the plaster to the water. Add the plaster gradually, sifting it through your fingers. Don't dump it in or the plaster will lump together, becoming difficult to mix. After you've sprinkled all the plaster into the water, let it *slake*—sit without stirring or agitating—for about 2 minutes. Then you can mix small batches by hand or use a power mixer for larger batches. This can be an electric drill with a propeller mixing attachment. In either case it is important to stir from the bottom of the mixture, keeping the hand or blade well below the surface. This helps drive out air bubbles without creating more of them. Air bubbles that do rise to the top can be skimmed off.

The more intense the mixing the faster the set. If mixing by hand, two to three minutes is fine. With a power tool, 1 minute should suffice. Any lumps found during stirring should be mashed up with your fingers. When the plaster resembles thick cream, it is ready to pour.

The Pour

Plaster needs to be poured smoothly, without splashing, so that no air bubbles are created or trapped by the pour. Pour the plaster to the very top of the container. Tap the sides of the container you are filling to bring air bubbles to the surface. Quickly pour any excess plaster into a waiting trash bag or can and rinse the mixing container in your rinse barrel.

When the plaster becomes mushy to the touch you can *screed* it by running a straightedge over the top to smooth it out. Do this in several passes, gently, a little at a time.

Drying

Water is the agent that hardens plaster, chemically bonding with it to form interlocking crystals. This is easily understandable when you consider that plaster is made by calcining gypsum, that is, heating the gypsum so that most of the chemically bound water is driven off. So the drying and hardening of plaster is really the *recrystallization* of gypsum or the recombining of water and gypsum molecules. Hardening plaster, therefore, expands and heats up. Put your hand on drying plaster and you can feel wet heat. When the plaster becomes cold to the touch again, the crystallizing process is over and the plaster mold can be removed from its forming container. The mold should be allowed to dry for a few days at room temperature. Don't put the new mold near an intense heat source, as it might cause the plaster to crumble. Infrared lights are okay. Be aware, though, that if the mold is too dry when you cast in it, it could cause air bubbles and pinholes in the clay.

Holding It In

Before mixing any plaster you should know what you want to do with it once it's mixed. Pouring it around models you've made from clay or some other material, or around objects you've found, will create *molds* of these models and objects that can then be used to repeat the forms in clay. Some of the enticing possibilities covered are hump molds, press molds, flat plaster slabs, one- and two-piece drain molds.

Your model should be set and ready before you mix any plaster. Whatever kind of mold or slab you make, some means of containing the plaster around the model or in the shape you want needs to be provided. The plaster should surround your model, not flow off your worktable, so outside forms are used to contain the poured plaster. These forms can be made in many ways, but are usually dependent on the size and shape of the mold being made. For shallow molds or slabs, plastic clay can be used. You can quickly *extrude* clay walls from a *hand extruder* or roll out *slabs* of clay (see chapter 3) and cut and assemble them into the desired configuration.

Make your molds and slabs on level, slick surfaces, such as glass, marble, linoleum, or polyurethaned wood. Make all joints tight by using strips of clay to seal them. You can also pour wet plaster into a rigid cardboard box. I wouldn't recommend using this method for anything too large—say over two gallons of plaster—as the force and dampness of the plaster could destroy the walls of the box before you could finish making a two-piece mold.

An easy retaining wall is made by circling a strip of strong nonabsorbent material that bends but won't collapse. The resulting cylindrical form open at both ends is called a *coddle*. Some of the possible materials to use are heavy plastic, heavy roofing paper, brass, and linoleum. Linoleum scraps are easy to get from a flooring dealer and make a cheap source for coddles. Warning: Don't try to bend cold linoleum, as it will crack. Warm it to at least room temperature. After it's been coiled, clamp your coddle with clothespins or wood-clamps and wind some wire or rope around it for firmness. Use strips of plastic clay to seal the joints between the coddle and the surface it's on. This prevents the plaster from leaking out the bottom and helps hold the coddle in place. The liquid plaster exerts a lot of pressure on your forms, so they need to be strong.

A *casting box* is another alternative, generally used for larger rectangular forms. A box form can be made from four plywood or particle-board sections cut to the desired dimensions for the model or form you are making a mold of. All boards should be sealed with shellac or its equivalent. In assembling a casting box, the boards should be placed so that one end of each board butts up against the face of another board. This helps strengthen the form. All outside joints are then sealed with plastic clay; rope or wire is tied around the box, tightened by the use of wedges. If the box form tends to move when you pour the plaster into it, you can use more clay around the outside or go to the trouble of using clamps. Most people making many molds clamp or wire the wood forms together so they can reuse them quickly and easily. But if you're not going to make a lot of molds you can just nail the boards together.

Sizing Up the Situation

After constructing outside forms for the plaster to be poured in, it is necessary to make sure the forms can be released from the hardened plaster, and that any model you pour over can also be released. Furthermore, in making two-or-more-piece drain molds, liquid plaster is poured over freshly hardened plaster and needs to separate perfectly from it. So, just before you are ready to mix a batch of plaster, you need to apply a *parting compound*, often called *sizing*, to all surfaces with which liquid plaster will come in contact.

The most commonly used parting material is liquid soap, which can be purchased at any craft-supply store. There are also some paste sizings available commercially that work quite well. Thirty-weight oil will also work just fine. Just remember the sizing should be done *immediately before* mixing the plaster, as it quickly loses its effectiveness.

There is usually no need to size wet clay or glass before plaster comes in contact with it. Actually the only time sizing is critically needed is when you pour fresh plaster against the hardened plaster of a model or piece(s) of a mold.

Before sizing plaster, make sure that it's damp or else you'll be sizing forever. If it's bone dry, dampen with a sponge. The separator can be applied to plaster with a soft brush or natural sponge. When using liquid soap, follow directions for diluting it, and apply in successive coatings. After each application, wait for the plaster to absorb the soap, and then apply more. You'll know when to stop when you see the plaster surface turn from dull to glossy. After the plaster reaches this glossy stage, stop sizing and, with a clean sponge or brush, clean off any soapsuds left by the operation. Any bubble or bead left on the sized plaster will prevent the liquid plaster from flowing into that space, so it's important to clean all sized surfaces. Avoid touching any of the sized plaster.

If any separator accidentally gets on the inside surface of a plaster mold used for casting slip clay, it will hinder the absorption of water from the clay slip and should therefore be removed. Do this with a clean cloth soaked in vinegar.

Plaster Molds

Now that some kind of a "do this before you do that" order has been established for using plaster, here are some of the possible ways to use it.

Press Molds

Press molds are usually used to produce detail elements or embellishments in clay for application to larger clay pieces. But buttons, beads, pins, and small objects can be made from press molds. As the name implies, plastic clay is *pressed* into the mold and is then immediately removed.

The simplest press mold is really a *stamp*. In this case, the mold is pressed into the clay rather than the clay being pressed into the mold.

Making Them   For small things like press molds, any containers already available will suffice, unless you really want to make your own. For example, you can take a muffin pan or twelve paper cups and place *face up* in six of the containers, one in each, a seashell, the letter *X* from an alphabet set, the key to a lock, a tooth, a quarter, and some raisins. All the objects are sized, as are the containers. (It is not necessary to size paper cups, though.) Plaster is mixed and poured into all twelve containers. When the plaster has cooled and set, all twelve pieces are removed (the paper cups can be torn away from the plaster) and the six pieces that had no models in them can then be carved into. Dentists' tools are great for this kind of carving, as well as for drawing directly in clay, but any pointed tool will do. You will then have twelve different press molds to play with, using them wherever you see fit.

One caution: if the models you use are very light, such as feathers or fishbones, you'll need to devise a way to make them stay down on the bottom instead of floating up on the wet plaster. One way is to glue them to the bottom with white glue or rubber cement. If the object is made of clay, it can be lightly wetted and pressed to the bottom surface, *gently*, so as not to disturb the design.

Using Them

Force plastic clay into the depression made by the model or carving, and press and smooth the back of the clay with a knife or spatula. Then carefully lift the clay out of the mold by inserting a needle tool slightly into the back of the clay and pulling. If the press-molded piece is to be an addition to a piece you are working on, it should be made from the same clay body and attached with slip. Colorants can then be added to the clay used for press molding for color variations.

Hump Molds

A hump mold is really any form that plastic clay can be draped over. It gives shape to the clay and supports it until dry enough to be removed without losing its given shape. Plas-

ter is a logical material to make the molds out of because of its ability to absorb moisture from the clay and hasten the drying process. The hump mold is usually used to do plate or platter forms, but the concept can be extended in many directions. Indeed, the hump doesn't have to be thought of as just a convex, positive shape that clay is draped over; it can also be a concave, negative shape that clay is pressed into. (This is, technically, a one-piece drain mold, but if you don't want to use slip clay, think of it as a dehumped mold.) The mold used with a jigger machine is essentially a hump mold (see "Jiggering," page 57).

Making Them

To make a positive hump form in plaster to drape clay over, you need a negative shape to pour the plaster into. Old bowls or platters that have the contour you want, woks, or the insides of hubcaps can make excellent instant forms for the plaster. If you're proficient on the potter's wheel, you can throw the plate or bowl shape you want, smoothing the inside wall carefully with a rib. Dry and bisque-fire the shape and then pour plaster into it. The plaster mold can be sanded smooth once it's hardened.

Plaster can be poured into a cavity that has been scooped, shaped, and smoothed out of wet sand.

A terrific contraption can be made from fabric and fishing line or wire. Cut a square of fabric a little larger than the size of the mold you want, then securely fasten a length of fishing line in each corner. Hang the four lengths of line from two poles stretched across sawhorses. Balance the lines and tie them so that the material hangs evenly above the ground. Now roll out a thick slab of clay and cut it into a circle or square the size of the mold you want. Center the clay slab as best you can in the material, which will begin to give with the clay's weight. By pulling on the four lines you can achieve any concave shape you want, from an almost flat slab to a severe bowl shape. Tie off the lines and let the clay dry in the material. After bisque firing, the clay is used as a mold for plaster.

To make a dehumped mold, the bisqued clay is turned over and the plaster is poured over it. In this case some kind of retaining wall needs to be used around the clay to keep the plaster from flowing away.

Using Them   You simply roll out slabs of clay and drape them over or into the plaster molds you have made. The outside rims of clay can be trimmed with a knife or a needle tool, and smoothed with a sponge. The clay can be cut into any shape you want while it's on or in a mold.

Drain Molds

Drain molds are designed to use deflocculated clay slip, the slip being poured into, then out of, the mold. The wall of the clay next to the plaster is allowed to build up to the thickness we want, and the excess slip clay is then poured out of the mold. It is possible to cast in one-piece molds provided they have *draft* and no *undercuts*.

Make Mine Draft   Any object that tapers from top to bottom, so that it is widest at the top and narrowest at the bottom, is said to have *draft*. An object can be turned over to accommodate this definition.

An object with draft will withdraw easily from a plaster mold it is cast into—provided it also has no *undercuts*. An undercut is an indentation or outcropping in the contour of a shape; undercuts prevent withdrawal of a casting from a mold. It is important to be able to conceptualize the shapes you want to cast in these terms, not just to determine whether they can be made into a one-piece drain mold, but because even in multiple-piece molds, each piece must be free from undercuts in order for the casting to release.

One-Piece Drain Molds   For simple shapes that have draft and no undercuts, a one-piece mold can be used. The dehumped molds made for plastic clay shapes are essentially one-piece drain molds and can be used as such (see Photoessay on Duane Ewing, page 107).

Making a one-piece drain mold of a simple object requires only one pour of plaster. Place the object on a level surface and build a coddle or casting box around it; then pour the plaster until it's about 2 inches above the top of the object. This can be a found object or something you make, perhaps by throwing a shape on the potter's wheel that can then be cast. In this case, use a flat bat made of plaster or sealed wood whose diameter is a couple of inches larger than the diameter of the bottom of the piece. The shape can be thrown solid, again remembering that any throwing marks or gouges in the clay will be reproduced in the mold. If you want them, great; if not, smooth the clay with ribs and sponge. The clay can also be sanded smooth after it has dried.

Two-or-More-Piece Drain Molds   When objects to be cast are complicated in shape, with undercuts and sharp angles, it is necessary to divide the mold up into pieces so that each piece conforms to the principles of draft and no undercuts. This requires studying the model with an eye toward the subsequent release of the clay casts from the mold. Turning the model on different axes may help resolve the problem, so that instead of the pieces of a mold parting on a horizontal axis, they separate laterally, or even at an angle to the axes.

To find the line of separation between two sections of an irregularly shaped model, rub indelible pencil on the outside edge of the vertical arm of a *carpenter's square*. Place the horizontal arm flat on the surface the model is resting on and move the model around so that the vertical arm's penciled edge touches the model. The pencil will make a line that traces along the high points of the model's contour. That is the line of separation. For three-or-more-piece molds it's up to your eye and experience to determine these lines.

Making Them   The procedure for making the piece mold is not difficult once you've figured out how to divide the model. It means blocking off all areas except the one piece that is being molded in plaster and doing this until all the pieces of the mold have been made. The easiest way to block off sections is with plastic clay.

When placing the model on a level surface in preparation for the plaster pour, it is important to keep the *base* of the model either perpendicular or parallel to the work surface. This ensures that the finished mold can have its base in a horizontal, level position when it is filled with slip clay and thus prevent air from being trapped in the mold. Air gets trapped when the slip is poured in at an angle.

With a pencil draw the line(s) of separation between the pieces of the mold on your model. For piece molds it is more convenient to use a separate and movable surface to pour plaster on, rather than a worktable, since the model needs to be turned frequently while plastic clay is used to block out areas not being cast in the first pour. Any sealed wood, plywood, or particle board at least ½ inch thick can be used. Cut it several inches larger than the size of the model about to be cast in plaster.

Place the model on a couple of wads of plastic clay on the baseboard. Casting from the mold later on will be much easier if you place the *base* of the model at one edge of the baseboard, either perpendicular or parallel to it. Look directly down at the model from above. You should be able to see every surface that is planned for the first piece of the mold. If you can't, keep turning the model on the clay wads, keeping the model base parallel or perpendicular to the work surface, until you can see all the right surfaces. If this isn't possible, you need to rethink your line(s) of separation, or perhaps you must add another section to the mold.

With the model in place, begin to build up plastic clay from the baseboard and add it until all that shows of the model is the first section to be cast in plaster. The top of the clay should be smoothed out all along the line of separation and extending to the edge of the baseboard. The sides of the clay build-up can be cut flush with the board.

Build a casting box around the model, flush with the baseboard. Remember that the top of the casting box should be about 2 inches above the highest point on the model. If your boards are higher than this, make a mark with a pencil so you'll know where to stop pouring plaster. Now size the model part that is showing and, if necessary, the side boards. The wet clay won't need sizing.

Mix and pour plaster into one corner of the casting box until you reach the tops of the boards or the mark you've made. After pouring, shake the table gently to bring any air bubbles to the surface.

When the plaster has cooled and hardened, the box can be removed and the entire clay, plaster, and baseboard complex turned over so it sits now on the just-hardened plaster. Remove the baseboard and clay build-up, leaving the model in the plaster. If there are only two pieces to the final mold there is no more clay build-up needed. If there are more than two pieces, you need to start building up clay and blocking out all areas except the second section to be cast in plaster and of course, the first section already cast.

With a curved knife or a spoon cut three small round tapering depressions in the just-cast plaster. These act as *keys* when you assemble the plaster mold and ensure that all the pieces realign themselves. Put one key in each of three corners or equidistant from each other. When the second pouring is done over these, the positives of these notches will be formed on the second section. Keys are made for every new section in a mold, so that all pieces are keyed with at least one other piece of the mold.

The casting box is rebuilt around the model, again two inches above the highest point. Both the exposed part of the model and the surface of the just-cast first piece need to be sized now before the second piece of the mold is poured. After fresh plaster is mixed and poured and dried, the two-piece mold is done. Continue on in this fashion for a more complicated mold.

If any clay sticks to the inside surface of the mold or if any nicks occur, they should be cleaned up immediately with sponge and sandpaper. Large nicks can be filled in with fresh plaster.

When making molds, be sure to keep in mind that you need a hole to get clay slip in and out of. This should be easy to take care of if the base of the model is cast in the position recommended. Refer to the photoessays on Duane Ewing and Will Herrera to see some other conditions.

Using Them

All the pieces of a mold are held tightly together either by large rubber bands or mold belts (both are available at supply stores) before the clay slip is poured into them. The mold is then set on the floor or a steady table with its access hole in a straight vertical position. Screened slip clay is poured into the hole and allowed to set up to a desired thickness. The excess slip is poured out. The clay casting then needs to dry in the mold. The time it takes for the slip clay to cast and for the casting to dry depends on how wet the mold was before casting, the thickness of the casting you want, and the nature of the slip. So the casting needs to be checked quite often to see how it's drying. The clay will begin to pull away from the mold wall when it's dry enough to remove from the mold. If you pull a mold apart too soon you will distort the casting.

After the casting is out of the mold, it needs to be cleaned. The lines or ridges resulting from the different pieces of a mold can be scraped down with a *fettling knife* or a flexible metal rib and sponged smooth.

"Untitled" by Richard Shaw

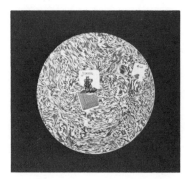

The large basement of his house in Fairfax, California, serves as Richard Shaw's studio. He stores most of his necessary tools and materials—powdered clays in bags stacked on wooden pallets, mixed moist clay stashed in covered plastic garbage cans, shelves stuffed with plaster molds, jars of commercial glazes and underglazes, bags of bulk china paints jammed into an old icebox, and one electric kiln—in the perimeter of the room. The rest of the studio is filled with large worktables.

Shaw has been working for the past couple of years with ceramic decals he's made from many of the bits and pieces that have drifted into his life: letters, cigarette packages, old photos, newspaper clippings, playing cards, and the like. He uses these on cast and handbuilt pieces and groups them on large plates. The use of many decals, cut and arranged on the plates, evokes personal remembrance and experience, and it displays his delight in having found design and color in those particular images.

When David Powers and I arranged to photograph him, Shaw had several plate commissions, and he wanted to do them in marbled clay. This marbling technique, a result of layering, cutting, and recombining colored clays, is also known as *neriage*.

Shaw forms his plates on a potter's wheel converted to a jigger machine, and after bisque and glaze firing, he applies china-paint decals. In the process, he used colored clays—white, blue, and red-brown. All were based on a high-fire porcelain clay body. Without any coloring additions to it, the porcelain will fire white. Richard added cobalt oxide to the formula to obtain the blue color, and used iron oxide and manganese dioxide for the red-brown. He did not weigh out the colorants when making up the colored clays, but rather added the oxides to the porcelain. From past experience, he judged his needs by the color in the still-wet clay. He did, however, fire samples of each clay to make sure he would get the color he wanted in the fired state.

Slabs are rolled out on material such as canvas or burlap, which stretches with them as they're rolled and gives when they shrink, thus helping to prevent cracking. The material is then used as a sling for turning the slabs over.

The clays were rolled out with a rolling pin to a thickness of about ¼ inch; several large slabs of each clay started the process. They were cut to similar dimensions and slip (made from the same clay body) applied between them before they were layered one atop another, in alternating colors. Another color can be added to the marbled pattern by using stain(s) or oxide(s) in the slip. In this case, pink stain #1 was used, although Shaw sometimes uses black slip for a high-contrast line in the pattern. By cutting the first stack in half again and again, and placing one half on top of the other and rerolling them with a rolling pin, the slabs of color eventually become thin lines.

Different marbling effects are achieved by cutting the stack into two or more parts and recombining the sections so that the clay lines are not parallel to each other. The stack can be cut and recombined in

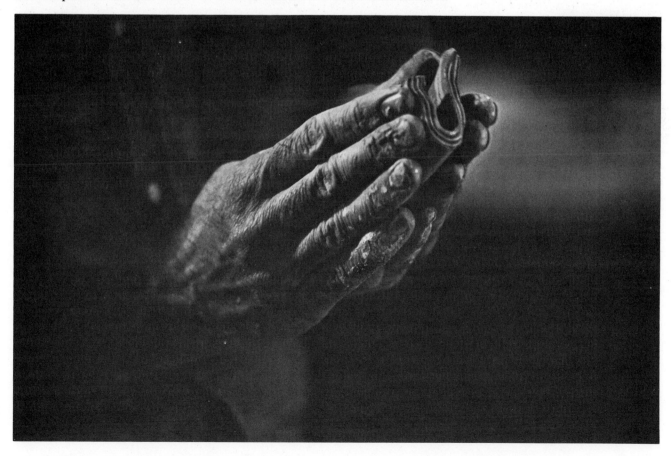

limitless ways. With a little experience you will be able to control the patterns. Eventually the stack is recombined into a shape somewhat larger than the diameter of the plate to be made. Shaw cut the final stack that he formed into three cross-section slabs, each large enough for the plate size he wanted. He used the same three colored clays in a different neriage technique to make another plate. In this case, instead of working the rolled slabs into one big stack, he cut and folded small individual pieces and then placed them together into a slab of the desired size.

The end result of either technique is a marbled clay slab about $^3/_8$ inch thick. This is then rolled a little thinner on a sheet of heavy plastic and cut into a circle about the diameter of the required plate. The plastic is used to lift the slab so it can be turned over onto the plaster mold. The slab is forcefully thrown down onto the wetted mold in order to make good contact and prevent air pockets from forming underneath.

The clay is then sponged with water and, while the wheel head is spinning, finger pressure is exerted down across the clay to secure it to the mold and check to make sure no air pockets remain.

Three or four passes are then made with the jigger arm, keeping the clay well lubricated with water. The outside edge is trimmed with a

needle tool and finished with a sponge to form the lip of the plate. The mold with the plate stuck to it is then moved from the wheel head and set aside to dry overnight. This jiggering process allows the inside surface of clay to remain undisturbed, preserving the marbled pattern. It also compresses the clay and helps prevent drying cracks.

The next day the not-quite-leather-hard plate and mold are placed back on the wheel head and white slip is brushed onto the entire back of the plate while the wheel is spinning. This slip is made from the porcelain clay body and need not be deflocculated. Any rough edges are smoothed out with a sponge and a rib.

After the slip has dried, a fired porcelain support ring, a little smaller in diameter than the plate itself, is placed on the back of the plate. Since the backs of the plates are left unglazed, this support ring can remain under the plate throughout the bisque and glaze firing to help keep it from slumping or distorting. The rings are made by throwing porcelain on a wheel into open cylinders of the necessary diameter and then firing them to maturity at cone 8. They need to be as tall as the plates to support them.

A wooden board is then placed on top of the ring, and by holding the mold from underneath and the board on top, the whole sandwich is turned over. The mold is removed and the plate is left right side up on its support ring.

It is at this point that Shaw begins to decide what the decal design is going to look like. To raise the decals slightly off the plates, he mounts them on very thin pieces of clay cut into the shapes he wants. These need to be attached to the plate now, before it gets too dry. Not all the decals are always given this clay backing, so Shaw can add others if he finds them necessary for the overall design.

To get the very thin slabs of clay, he pours a deflocculated slip, made from the porcelain clay body, onto a plaster slab. By lifting and tilting the plaster slab, he distributes the slip in a thin sheet over the slab. When this dries sufficiently, he pulls the entire sheet off the plaster, and from this thin piece of clay, he cuts the shapes he wants with an X-acto knife, aided by templates. The templates are the shapes of decals and have been made about 15 percent larger than the actual decals to allow for drying and firing shrinkage in the clay body. After cutting out the shapes, Shaw usually tears or roughly cuts them to maintain the fragmented quality he wants the decals to have. These paper-thin cutouts are then positioned on the plate; the visual relationships are worked out before they are scored, slipped, and attached to the plate.

Shaw then uses a metal rib and a single-edge razorblade to scrape the surface of the now leather-hard plate. This brings out a sharper image of the marble pattern. After the scraping is complete, the plate is set aside on its support ring, covered with plastic, and allowed to dry slowly. This may take several days to a week, depending on how tightly the plastic is wrapped.

When dry, the plate and ring are placed in the electric kiln and bisqued to cone 07.

The plate and ring are then removed from the kiln, and the clay cut-outs are given a thin application of transparent glaze. The plate on its ring is put back in the electric kiln and fired to cone 8. The firing and cooling are done very slowly, over a period of two days, to prevent cracking due to quartz inversion.

The fired plate is then ready for the decals. First the glazed cut-out shapes are traced with tracing paper and pencil. The decals themselves are cut to those shapes with an X-acto knife, then soaked in water, and finally applied to the matched clay shape. If any other decals are added—that is, to the unglazed portion of the plate—white glue is put on and allowed to set up on the portion of the plate where the decals will go. The decals are then immersed in water and applied on the glue. The plate and decals are dried for at least twenty-four hours and then the plate is put into the kiln (the support ring is no longer necessary) and fired to cone 018. The kiln is cooled slowly.

There are often other additions made to the plates: a thin oxide wash can be airbrushed over a decal to make it appear aged, shadows can be airbrushed in, or a shadowy hand laid down.

Though the clay body Shaw used for these plates is high-fire, all the techniques and processes discussed can be done with low-fire clays. But he demonstrates that low-fire glaze firings can be done on high-fire clay bodies. The color photo of a finished marbled plate is in Plate 39.

Other Ways to Make It

Toward Working

There's no limit to the ways of working with clay. Mexican folk potters make bowls by slapping clay onto their elbows. A high-rise construction worker discovers the joys of clay in a night class and dreams of dropping 500-pound slugs of plastic clay from the top of a skyscraper into the cleared street below, imagining the impressions and contours the thudding clay would pick up.

Whether through cultural necessity or sheer whimsy, clay inspires personal response. In spite of the technical innovations and equipment available to the contemporary craftsman, clay still must be "handled"—touched, worked, pushed, and pulled by hands controlled by emotions and imagination. Despite the use of molds, wheels, and tools, clay is essentially whatever you are willing to discover from it while loving it, hating it, surprising it, and being surprised by it. A personal *way* of working develops naturally. Learning new techniques and methods is only an aid toward that development.

Once clay becomes a constant companion of your clothes and thoughts, you will discover new ways to work, just by looking or at least *seeing* in terms of clay.

Unless otherwise indicated, all of the techniques described in this chapter make use of *plastic clay*, rather than deflocculated slip. As in the mastery of any endeavor, timing and attention to procedural order are critical: the horse before the cart, the run before the leap. Clay is a remarkable material, willing to do almost anything, *if* it's done when the clay is ready, not just at your convenience. Most of what I'm saying here applies to the relative wetness or dryness of the clay. The wetter the clay (without getting mushy) the more plastic and malleable it is, and therefore the easier to get into those shapes and contours that were so readily sketched on paper; yet, when wet, it is less likely to *hold* those shapes. Here is where you need to be able to devise technical solutions. Some potters have developed techniques for throwing on the wheel without using any water for lubrication. Using only fingertips while pulling ensures that the clay doesn't absorb any moisture and weaken. Large, thin pots are the result. The application of texture and incised lines, the joining of clay to clay, are only a few of the procedures that require personal experience to know *when* to do them. And you must order your working so that one procedure doesn't obliterate its precedents, nor make it impossible to continue with other steps. I've done several large slab pieces with 2-inch letters stamped into the sides, which had to be pressed into the wet clay slabs *before* the slabs were put together; otherwise the clay would have been too dry to get a clear, deep impression.

Getting Attached

Since there are many approaches to forming clay, much work is done by using multiple techniques. When combining cast pieces with thrown forms or extruded parts with slabs, you must be careful to join the parts at the proper time and also take precautions to prevent the parts from pulling away from each other during drying and firing. The wetter the clay parts, the better they will adhere to each other. Also the pieces should be about the same wetness when joined, and be kept wet after joining. The principles discussed in chapter 1 about the drying of clay are even more critical here. Wrap joints in plastic and keep pieces in a damp box or under plastic. The length of time needed to dry a piece depends on its size. Thrown sinks with $\frac{1}{2}$-inch-thick walls and attached slab backsplashes I let dry under plastic for two to three weeks.

Whenever one piece of clay is attached to another—even if it's a very small press-molded decoration being applied to a large form—both pieces should be *scored* at their points of attachment (roughed up with a fork or serrated rib or the equivalent) and thick slip dabbed on at least one of the surfaces. *Slip* here refers to the plastic clay body mixed with water; no deflocculant is necessary. Put enough pressure on the pieces so that their clay molecules really intermingle. Unless *they* are convinced they are of the same piece, cracking is inevitable.

If you are not making a functional piece, you can design parts that can be fired separately and assembled afterward with epoxy or some other space-age goo.

Extrusion

Extrusion is the process of forcing clay through a *die*—like using decorating tubes to ornament a cake.

Small decorating sets include a 3-inch-long tube, a plunger, and various dies, useful for small detail work. The dies usually include several sizes of round holes, which make wonderful clay coils, squares, half-circles, and triangles. A solid die with tiny holes punched in it is perfect for representing human hair or animal fur. (You can get the same results with a garlic press or hand-cranked food mill.)

A *pugmill* is a machine that mixes and often de-airs clay and then forces it out the end of a long compacting tube. Generally, it is used industrially only to make clay, that is, to get a homogeneous plastic clay body ready for use in some other process. Sometimes, however, a die is fitted to the end of the extruding nozzle to form tiles, sewer pipe, and other simple shapes.

There are now many extruders on the market scaled down to a size convenient, useful, and affordable in the studio. These are much larger than the decorating sets and much smaller than a pugmill. They consist of a tube about 6 inches in diameter and a piston/plunger device operated by hand. A removable cap at one end holds a die in place. Wedged plastic clay is loaded in at the top end of the tube and the plunger device seated on top of the clay. When pressure is exerted on the plunger handle, clay is forced out the bottom of the tube, passing through the die and taking its shape.

Dies can be made out of clay, Masonite, or steel. Since there is considerable force exerted on the die during extrusion, particularly if the clay is on the stiff side, Masonite or steel is usually the best choice for die material—which means that you may have to have your dies made in a machine shop or cut them yourself using drills, torches, and grinders to get the shapes you want. To make clay dies all you need are your hands and a few tools. Any clay die should be at least ¾ inch thick, dried slowly, and fired to its maturing temperature. A glaze will usually add compressive strength to the clay, but be careful not to destroy the detail of your work by getting the glaze on too thick.

With these extruders you can make hollow tubes or rectangles as thin-walled as you want. Be sure that all metal dies are filed and sanded smooth around all edges, since a small burr can tear the extruded clay. To make a tube die, start with a disc of ¹⁄₁₆-inch sheet metal (though metal a little thicker can certainly be used if you're scrounging). This disc should seat itself into the retaining cap of your extruder. Cut, punch, or drill a hole the size you want your tube to be in the center of the disc. A jeweler's saw will cut ¹⁄₁₆-inch sheet metal fairly readily, if you drill a hole just inside the edge of the space you intend to cut out in order to give the blade a place to start. After this hole is cut, center another, smaller disc of metal in it. The size of this disc will determine how thick a wall your tube will have. For example, if you start with a 6-inch disc, and cut a hole 4 inches in diameter within it, and then use a 3½-inch disc in the hole, you will be extruding a 4-inch-diameter tube whose walls are ¼ inch thick.

Now the two discs need to be connected or bridged so that the space between them (the wall of the tube) is left totally unobstructed. Two U-bolts will solve the problem. One foot of a U-bolt is welded to the inside disc and the other foot is welded to the outer disc. If you prefer to bolt them, you can drill holes in appropriate places and secure the bolts with washers and nuts. Two bolts will provide sufficient rigidity and strength. This principle of die construction can be applied to hollow cubes, rectangles, and polygons. Set the die in place with the U-bolts inside the extruder, load the clay in the tube, and extrude it through the die.

Extruded clay can be used as handles for cups, planters, and casseroles, and for picture frames and kiln furniture. Vessels can also be made from extruded tubes and rectangles. Even workable musical instruments have been fashioned from tubes. Bill Albright's "Erecto-pyre," Plate 34, makes use of extruded stick forms.

Coils

One of the oldest methods of forming clay pieces uses coils or ropes of clay laid one atop another, building a vessel coil by coil from the bottom up. The coils are made by rolling clay between hands or under fingertips on a work surface, or with the aid of a hand extruder and round die. These coils are then usually welded together and scraped smooth so that no marks are seen, although they can be left for special effects. If the coil marks are left in, a variety of patterns can be gotten by changing the diameters of the coils used and the directions they're placed in. Use colored clays to further accentuate coil patterns.

Coils can also be used to add height to a

thrown pot. Let the top of the pot dry enough to support the weight of more clay, and then attach as many coils as are needed to finish the shape. These can be left as "coils" or finished on the wheel as a continuation of the thrown section.

In my own work, and the work of many others, coil-like pieces are used as additions to thrown, slab, or cast forms, and not only to enclose a volume of space or create vessels. I use a lot of tapered coils: large for legs on thrown forms, and small for decoration and handle shapes (see "Altered Piece #1," Plate 32). Instead of just rolling out a straight coil, I'll work one end a little more than the other to taper it. Away from the wheel, the slab roller, extruder, and molds, I can get closer to a piece, working mostly by addition. I often make preliminary sketches, but when I start to work in three dimensions I have to pay attention to what the clay is telling me and go from there. When I'm finished with a piece, there are a myriad clusters of clay wads, balls, strips, curlicues, and hunks strewn all over my studio, rejected for their betters. (I classify all of these under *coils* so I won't have to have a section called "Bits and Pieces.")

Slabs

Slab construction is the process of forming and joining pieces of rolled-out, flat clay. Slabs are used to construct individual forms, component forms, or additions to pieces constructed in another way. Don't think of slabs being used only to make boxes, for they are really just starting points in a very malleable medium. Remember, for instance, that slabs can be draped over hump molds to form bowls and plates.

Making Slabs

The simplest way to form slabs of clay is to throw a wad of plastic clay against a floor or table, retrieve it, turn it 90 degrees, and throw it down again. Repeat this process until the piece of clay has stretched into a slab as thin as you desire, even paper-thin. With a little practice you can start to throw some good-sized slabs, stretching out 3 or 4 feet. This is a good method if the clay thickness need only be approximate.

Slabs of clay can be rolled out with a rolling pin or length of pipe as if the clay were pie-crust dough. If you need slabs of a particular thickness, find some wood slats of that thickness and roll the slab between the slats so that each end of the roller eventually rolls on a slat.

The following is a good method for making many slabs at once without having to roll them out: Set a block of plastic clay between two rows of stacked slats, each slat the same thickness as the desired slab of clay. Then pull a sharp cutting wire taut across the two top slats and back through the slug of clay. Then remove the top slat on each pile, and pull the wire across the next two slats. Repeat this process until the final slats are reached. Good cutting wires, by the way, can be made from monofilament fishing line, or thin wire, my preference being a stainless violin E-string. Tie each end of the wire to a washer or piece of wood dowel with holes drilled in it to provide handles for your wire.

Slab rollers, a new piece of equipment designed solely for their named purpose, can produce slabs of uniform thickness quickly and evenly. There are two types on the market, those built like etching presses with stationary double rollers, and those with a single moving roller. The latter requires its own table surface and works on the same principle as rolling a slab between two wooden slats, while the double-roller models can be adapted to any studio work surface and then be stored elsewhere when not in use. The single-roller table models come with many shims of various thicknesses, and slab thickness is adjusted by taking these shims out or putting them in. With the double-roller models, you adjust the distance between the two rollers to adjust the thickness of the slab.

As you have probably realized by now, the

stiffness of the plastic clay you roll relates to the type of work you are doing. If the slabs are to be cut into squares and assembled as a box, then you need stiff clay so that the slabs will be strong enough to stand on their own. A slab that is going to be draped around some interior form, or simply bent around and joined to itself to form a cylinder, needs to have the plasticity of wetter clay.

The stiffer the clay, the less tendency it has to stick to the surface you are rolling it on. The clay can be rolled on boards and then set aside to allow the slabs to stiffen without disturbing them. Sometimes rolling clay on fine grog or sand helps prevent the slabs from sticking to the work surface. Cloth, plastic, and even newspaper are often used for the same purpose. It is also good to keep in mind that you can texture clay while you are rolling slabs by working on canvas, burlap, or weeds, whose textures are then incorporated into the surface of the slabs.

What to Do with a Slab

Two things become very clear when you begin to work with *large* slabs: the just-rolled slab is usually too wet to hold a shape when placed upright on one of its edges (even if you're working with stiff clay), *and* once the slab does get dry enough to hold its shape, it often becomes too hard to attach to other pieces of clay without threat of the joint's cracking during drying and firing.

This dilemma can be resolved in several ways, not the least of which is patience and attention to your clay. Some shapes will support themselves once all the slabs are connected. The trick is getting the first two slabs together. This may call for more than one pair of hands, or require waiting until the slabs *are* dry enough to support themselves, then wetting down the edges where they will be connected, and making sure to *score*, *slip*, and *compress* the joining surfaces firmly. In addition, it is wise to weld a coil of clay into the back of any seam by working the clay into the joint with a finger or wooden modeling

tool. After the piece is assembled, spray it with water from a plant mister and cover it with plastic.

Another solution to slab-construction problems calls on the use of support systems, both internal and external. Basic internal support of the clay utilizes grogs and fillers in the clay body. (See chapter 1.)

Another technique, developed by Daniel Rhodes, makes use of fiberglass cloth. Slabs are built by dipping pieces of the cloth in deflocculated slip and piling them one atop another until the desired thickness is reached. Rhodes states: "A very open-weave cloth must be used, and one which has not been coated with plastic. Light fiberglass cloth of the type made for sheer draperies has been found to be suitable. Tough slabs of great tensile strength both in the plastic and in the dry state may be made from fiberglass cloth and deflocculated slip. . . . A thick slip containing no more than about 35 percent water has been found to be suitable. Slips made with water and clay alone, without deflocculant, cannot be used because they will have too great a shrinkage and will lack density."

With this kind of internal support large, thin slabs will maintain their shapes whether they are used in symmetrical or asymmetrical forms. Look at John Bobeda's kite in Plate 29. By extending Rhodes's technique and incorporating others, Bobeda has created some breathtaking forms. He starts with a clay body made up of 50 percent kaolin and 50 percent talc, to which he adds about 20 percent (by weight) of fiberglass shreds. This body is then deflocculated. Later several pieces of fiberglass cloth are dipped in the slip and laminated together. Since these slabs exhibit no measurable drying shrinkage, Bobeda ruled out plaster as a mold material, opting for molds made of paper, plastic, and cloth. To prevent slumping during firing, Kaowool (a refractory fiber) and wooden struts are used inside the forms. The wood burns away during firing and the Kaowool is later removed. The forms are fired to cone 05 and left unglazed.

The kite form depends on internal support from the fiberglass shreds and cloth, as well as external support from molds, Kaowool, and wood. Bobeda has been very resourceful. (You will be looked on as resourceful when the new things you try actually work; otherwise you're considered *desperate*.) External support systems can be as simple as pushing a cardboard box against the side of a piece to keep it from falling over. For smaller pieces, the clay can be rolled on plastic (trashcan liners, etc.), so that the plastic backing helps to support the clay during forming and drying.

Wooden templates can be used to make large rectangular or polygonal forms that are clean-edged and free from distortion. Let's say you want to build a 2-foot cube with an open top. The clay walls for this piece should be at least ½ inch thick and highly grogged. We'll need five slabs: a bottom and four sides. The bottom will be a 24-inch square; two of the sides measure 23 inches wide by 23½ inches tall; the other two are the same height, but 24 inches wide. You are using a support system made from ⅜-inch plywood or particle board. The idea is to support each clay slab by sandwiching it between two boards, thus making the wet clay functionally rigid and therefore transportable.

Cut four plywood boards to the exact dimensions of the slab sides of the form. The slabs can then be rolled out directly on the boards or lifted onto the boards after forming. In the latter case, it is wise to reroll the slab lightly on the board to remove any air pockets lurking below. Then trim the slabs flush with the sides of the boards.

Before the slabs are put on the boards, however, some thin separating material should be laid on the boards. Plastic or newspaper will do just fine. This will allow the boards to pull away from the clay when you want to remove them.

Cut four more plywood boards for the front of each side slab. These boards should be smaller than the slabs themselves so that enough clay is exposed at the sides and bottom to allow for the joining of the slabs. Again, use some separating material between them.

Drill four holes, one near each corner of the smaller top board, through each of the four plywood-paper-clay-paper-plywood sandwiches. Then, using washers and nuts, inset and fasten each bolt. Now you can pick up each slab in order to join them together.

This is the time to call a friend. For a project of this magnitude you deserve some assistance. First, score and slip the entire perimeter of the base slab and the bottom edge of one of the side slabs. Then pick up this first side and slide it into place so that it sits on one edge of the base. Have your friend hold this in place while you score and slip the bottom and sides of the second slab and stand it on the base at a right angle to the first side. If you have cut your inside forms small enough, the corners of the slabs will meet. Later, these corners can be reinforced and trimmed neatly with straightedges and ribs.

The third and fourth sides are done in like manner, scoring and slipping and joining at corners. Once the piece is put together it is pretty much self-supporting so there is no need to keep the forms in very long. After the bolts and forms are removed, plug the holes made by the bolts with plastic clay, smooth all the seams, and work clay coils into the inside edges of all joints.

The use of an interior support system for enclosed forms can foster potential problems. Drying usually means shrinkage of the clay, and with enough shrinkage the plywood forms can get wedged in, making them impossible to get out. Once that happens, continued shrinkage would create enough pressure to crack all the joints. So don't let any piece you form with this method get too dry before pulling out the plywood forms.

If you can manage to get your slabs together without interior supports, and the interior space of the piece isn't functional, then you can use a clay-body support system, made up of interior walls or extruded tubes run between the perimeter walls of the piece. In this way all the clay shrinks at the same rate and precludes cracking.

Another solution using interior support for large asymmetrical forms was developed by David Middlebrook. He sews large shapes out of cloth (double-knit stretch fabric) and then stuffs them with vermiculite. Clay slabs are wrapped around the stuffed material, which supports the clay during drying. Vermiculite has the ability to give good support and yield to the shrinking clay at the same time. After the clay dries, the vermiculite is either dumped or vacuumed out. (See the photoessay on page 60.)

The Potter's Wheel

The potter's wheel is still the mainstay for many studio artisans. Ten years ago, all studio ceramics centered around the wheel, which discouraged a lot of people from working with clay because they couldn't master throwing. Hopefully by now we've learned that the wheel is only one of many approaches to dealing with clay.

Only two homilies before continuing: If being able to throw is your heart's desire, then find good instructors and study with them. Wheel work is a discipline, and like any other, it requires practice—every day for at least an hour or two. There are a lot of books that deal with throwing and they can be helpful, but the potter's wheel requires physical coordination as well as intuition, and an experienced guide makes the process of learning to throw much easier.

If you do get good at throwing and crave doing monumental pieces but still can't center 50 pounds of clay, try another technique—perhaps throwing in sections as Bill Abright does (see the photoessay on page 125), or getting off the wheel entirely and doing handbuilding. Don't frustrate your ideas by getting locked into one restrictive mode of working.

Jiggering

Jiggering is a process that makes clay shapes by using a mold for its inside form and a template for its outside form. It is one way a potter's wheel can be put to use in the studio.

The clay on the mold needs to be revolving on the wheel when the template is applied to it. Jiggering is essentially a throwing operation, except you get a lot of mechanical help. At a commercial level, special jigger machines cost many thousands of dollars and turn out hundreds and even thousands of pieces a day, but for the studio person who wants several smooth plate forms, the potter's wheel can be transformed into a simple jigger machine.

Jiggering plates is fairly easy and straightforward (recall the photoessay on Richard Shaw, page 40).

1. Attach a mold of the inside of the plate to the wheel head.

2. Drape a rolled slab of clay of uniform thickness over the mold.

3. With the wheel going, use a lever arm to lower a template of the outside of the plate onto the rotating clay. Use water to lubricate the clay during the operation.

Making It

Leonard Skuro of Los Angeles used an old potter's wheel to construct a jiggering outfit. The following is based on his experience: The basic idea of a jiggering machine is to have a *lever arm*—to which the outside template will be attached—swinging down over the middle of the wheel head. The arm should be long enough to reach beyond the front of the wheel head and fixed at a point at the back of the wheel from which it can pivot up and down. Skuro made the brace and lever arm out of wood, but they can be made of flat stock metal or even steel pipe. The braces that sandwich the lever arm are attached to the wheel's table.

There are really only two critical alignments that need to be made, and you should consider them while designing your jigger setup: The template blade should hit the spinning clay so that it is parallel to it and the wheel head and also is aligned with the mold underneath it.

Both of these requirements suggest that the template blade be adjustable, to allow you to position the template perfectly, not just for one plate form but for many forms. If you look at the photograph of Richard Shaw's jiggering setup (page 45), you'll see that the lever arm can be moved up or down between its supports, providing a rough positioning for the blade. The fine tuning is done where the template blade fits onto the lever arm, so it can move up or down and forward and backward on the arm. Skuro accomplished this by using slide holes in the arm and blade so that the blade could be positioned before being bolted to the arm.

The templates themselves were made from 3/16-inch flat stock steel, cut with a band saw and smoothed with a grinder and files. It is a lot easier if you make the template out of cardboard or matboard first, get the shape you want, and then use that as a pattern on the steel. The contact edge of the template should be beveled, not left flat. This cuts down on the surface area dragging on the clay, thus reducing the friction and possible trouble from vibrations. The steel templates are then mounted onto a 1/2-inch piece of wood cut the same shape as the template, so that only the cutting edge is not backed by wood. This will help minimize any vibrations during jiggering. After being aligned with the mold and clay, the wood-backed template is then attached to the lever arm with bolts.

The template is made of half the outside of the form—a profile, really, of the outside shape from its center to its rim (like all things done on the wheel, the form is basically a circle). The rotation of the wheel assures that all of the clay is profiled by the template. Thus the surface area of template hitting the clay is minimized. Since the front of the lever arm gives the most power and control, the template is attached to come in contact with the front to the center of the spinning form.

The template shape can be designed on paper, but it's best to make a model first and easiest to make a clay model. If you want to be precise, remember to account for shrinkage when making models and planning your

pieces. For example, if you wanted to end up with a fired plate 20 inches in diameter and are using a clay body that shrinks 10 percent when dried and fired for your model, you'd have to make the wet model 24.7 inches, since both the model and then the clay plate made from it will each shrink 10 percent. Skuro chose to make a wooden model of the desired plate and then form the template off the large wooden model.

The Mold

Skuro made two templates—from the inside and outside of his wooden model—so that he could jigger the hump mold form that would be the inside shape of the plate.

First he keyed a round polyurethaned piece of wood, 1/2 inch thick, to the wheel head with three pins—meaning that the three pins imbedded into the round bat were snugly fit into three holes in the wheel head, securing the bat to the head without any wiggling. (Other systems can certainly be devised to accomplish the same effect.)

With the bat in place on the wheel head, he tacked a 3-inch-wide strip of stainless steel around it. (You ought to recognize this as a coddle—see page 34.) The pins or bolts in the bat should be long enough to stick up through the top of the bat about an inch and a half. This helps secure the plaster to the bat, so the bat can serve as the means of attachment to the wheel head.

The plaster was then mixed and poured to the top of the steel band. As soon as the plaster started to set, the band was removed and the jigger arm with the inside template was brought down on the plaster while the wheel continued to spin. This needs to be done quickly and steadily before the plaster hardens all the way. It's a rather messy operation, but you can use a metal rib and a sponge to finish the plaster surface and make it even smoother.

With the mold in place, and the outside template on the jigger arm, you are ready to make plates. Roll out a slab of clay and drape it over the mold. Don't use stiff clay. Make sure there is no air trapped between the clay and the mold. Take a wet sponge and, with the wheel going, press down on the clay, running your hand from the center to the front lip, securing it to the mold. Trim off any excess at the lip with a needle tool. Then bring the jigger arm down against the rotating clay in several passes. The amount of vibration encountered will tell you how much water is needed to keep the clay lubricated and how much pressure you can apply with the jigger arm. When the form has dried a bit, the outside lip can be finished with a sponge.

"Big-Game Hunter" by David Middlebrook

David Middlebrook spent a year building a new 1,600-square-foot studio in Los Gatos, California, mostly from used lumber and old windows and skylights. The studio is one room with wooden flooring and white sheet-rocked walls. One animated night he described the studio as his ship in which he would sail unchartered and unrecorded places. His metaphor was clear as he stood at the bow of his ship looking out the huge slanted windows that face the Santa Cruz Mountains and up into the starry night above. Middlebrook wanted an expansive, clean space to work in, both because of the scale he works in and because he wanted to have a better idea of what they'll look like in a gallery while his pieces are still in the studio. He wanted the large space with white walls without losing his personal environment, therefore the old redwood trim and the special glass alcove for a cactus garden. The clay process doesn't happen at a gallery level—that's some-

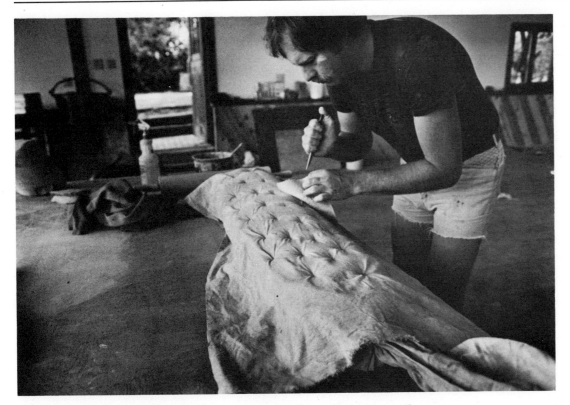

thing between the maker and his material. The gallery turns the process into objects. Middlebrook just wanted to have a better sense of what that did to his pieces while they were still in his own space.

When David Powers and I arrived, Middlebrook was just completing a large worktable. The piece for this book would be the first work done in the studio, a christening of sorts. He had been commissioned by a friend of his to do a large piece, and his adrenalin was urging him to do something spectacular.

The piece started as a drawing in Middlebrook's sketchbook. Objects that were already in his ceramic "vocabulary" would be incorporated with objects that held personal meaning between the two friends. The drawing was an idea sketch, not a blueprint; the piece would be changed several times in the process of making it. This is a difficult step. It is hard to let go of a *concept* long enough to see whether the *form* works well without it. There would be a lot of personal references in this piece that only Middlebrook and his friend would understand, and yet it also had to work for people who knew nothing about those references.

The elements in the sketch were: a stool, overgrown with cactus; a derby hat; and a pair of glasses, one side of which was covered with cactus, the other side of which was a pool rack with pool balls. Of all these elements, only the pool balls would be cast; the rest would all be fabricated by slab construction.

First Middlebrook constructed the elements that make up the stool. His usual method for doing slab work is to use forms made by stuffing material and pantyhose with vermiculite. The vermiculite-stuffed forms provide an internal support system for any clay shapes wrapped around

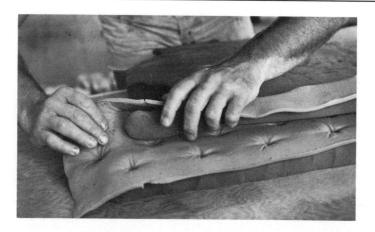

them. The vermiculite also gives with the clay as the clay shrinks, thus preventing cracking during drying.

Middlebrook made many tubular elements for the stool because he didn't know how many he'd need until he started putting them together—and that's a frustrating time to run out of pieces. He wanted the stool itself to be 34 inches tall. To start, balls of plastic clay of about 6 pounds were wedged and thrown onto the table to stretch them into slabs about ½ inch thick. Each slab was then put onto a piece of material and thinned to about ¼ inch with a rolling pin. A large piece of material sewn into a tube shape was filled tightly with vermiculite. The bag was tied off at its loose end and flattened out onto the table. The slab of clay was draped onto the bag and covered with a thin piece of canvas. Middlebrook then took a small piece of canvas and a wooden tool and went up and down the canvas punching depressions in it, which transferred through the two pieces of canvas to the clay. The vermiculite underneath gave with the punches so that holes were not made in the clay, only puckered depressions that give the look of cactus. For this piece however, Middlebrook used the bulging instead of the depressed side out. With the first slab still on the vermiculite form, Middlebrook pulled out an army of pantyhose to make long narrow tubes whose shape he could control by the amount of vermiculite he put in them. The open end of the pantyhose leg was tied off in a slip knot that would pull out easily when he was ready to empty it.

The slab on the big bag was rolled over onto a foam pad and the pantyhose form was laid in the center of it. The slab was then rolled over around the form and scored, slipped, and joined together to form a tapering tube. By pinching off sections of the stuffed form, he created a tapering, gnarled form in clay. Middlebrook made four legs and many other smaller elements to serve as supports and ladder rungs. While the clay was on the vermiculite form, he jarred it on the table to give it more of a cactuslike character. The tubes on their forms were then laid on foam pads to dry. When they were dry enough for assembly, he pulled the knot out of the pantyhose, dumped the vermiculite back into its container, and pulled the pantyhose through one end of the clay tube.

Because of this technique, Middlebrook is able to build monumental pieces rather quickly, using a clay body he doesn't grog or add anything

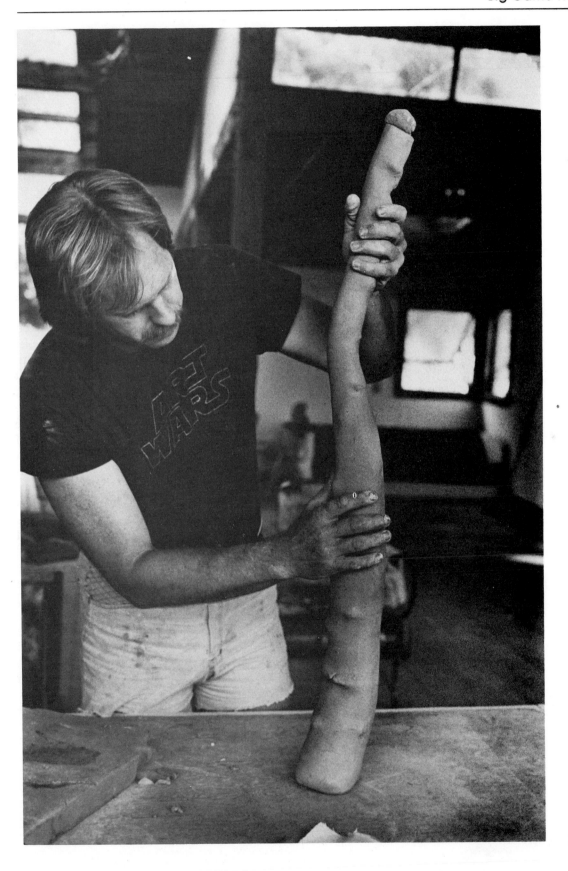

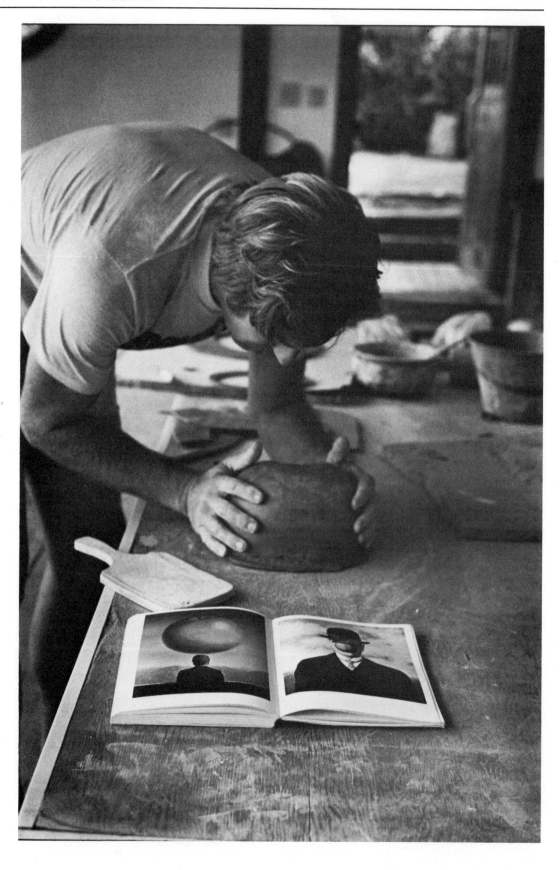

to. The stool was built, dried, and bisqued in a week. For a piece of this size, that's remarkable time. I want to point out that Middlebrook spends a lot of time and effort scoring, slipping, and smoothing every joint he makes, which is why he doesn't get much cracking at all in these large complicated works.

The two sections of the stool, each section comprised of two legs connected by cactus rungs, were assembled separately. Because of their irregular shapes, Middlebrook always supported the pieces on foam padding while he worked on them. All the joints and seams he made were smoothed out by running a fettling knife over a piece of cloth on the seam.

While working on one section, he broke one of the legs in two. To repair it, he made a sleeve that fit inside the two broken pieces, scored and slipped the outside of the sleeve and the inside of the leg near the break, and forced all three pieces together. He added a coil of clay to the joining seam on the outside of the leg and worked that with a fettling knife, finally hiding any trace of the break by rubbing the knife over the cloth at the seam. He covered the two sections with plastic and set them aside.

Making the most of his materials, Middlebrook used the seat of a pair of pantyhose stuffed with vermiculite as a form for the seat of the stool. The same textured-slab technique was used to produce two seats (the extra in case one cracked). These were set aside to dry.

Middlebrook then focused on constructing the derby hat. Again he stuffed the seat of a pair of pantyhose with vermiculite to serve as the form for the crown of the hat. He draped a slab of plastic clay over the vermiculite form, and, to get a tight shape, put the clay and form on a board and dropped them onto the table from about 5 feet in the air. This stirred up a lot of dust but stretched the clay around the form. Then he used a rubber kidney to smooth out the clay, rolled out a slab of clay, and cut the oval shape of the hat rim. These were put aside to firm up.

To make surface wood impressions, Middlebrook threw thin slabs of clay against the table and then, on the final throw, against a piece of rough 2-by-10-inch fir board. The clay slabs were left with the knots and grains of the wood. They would give the appearance that the stool

was at one time made of wood and had been overgrown by mutant cactus. Several wood pieces were made: when the slabs were almost leather-hard, he cut them into the necessary shapes, and beveled their edges, and scored, slipped, and joined them together. Then part of one leg and a rung on one section of the ladder were replaced with "wooden" pieces.

To accentuate this small corner of wood—and to give the stool a little character—Middlebrook made it appear as if the leg and the shaky rung had been splinted. Clay nails seemingly split the wood and a thin slab of clay acted as a piece of tin to fasten the splint to the leg. He used a stiff brush on some parts of the wood to make it appear worn and dinged from age and use.

The stool seat was then finished with a slab underside and one corner was replaced with a piece of "wood."

Back under plastic went the seat and stool parts. Out came the crown and brim of the derby. By now Middlebrook had borrowed a pool rack from his neighbor to serve as his model for the eyeglass frame. But he also knew that he wanted the rack to sit on the derby in the finished piece, so he used the real rack to make a depression in the still-wet clay crown for the to-be-constructed clay pool rack to sit in. Middlebrook then joined the crown and brim, working the brim into a curved shape with his fingers. He made a hatband by rolling a very thin slab of clay on corduroy material, beveling the two outside edges of the band to make it appear much thinner than it really is. After he attached it to the hat, he waxed the band with *wax resist* to slow down its drying and prevent it from cracking.

Out from under plastic came the seat and two stool sections. Middlebrook tied the back section to a chair so it was standing up in the position he wanted. This freed him to lean the second section into the first at the proper angle and attach the two with a lot of scoring, slipping, and clay additions. He made two holes in the bottom of the seat so it could fit over the two knobs that joined the four legs at the top of the stool.

The stool dried for four days, then Middlebrook unstacked the electric kiln, which made it easier to set the stool in. He spread grog on the kiln floor before the stool was loaded. The grog allowed the clay to give and move a little while it was firing and shrinking. If the bottom legs were stationary, the strain of shrinking would tend to warp the piece. He then carefully stacked the kiln sections around the stool again and fired the stool to cone 02.

Several small cracks developed in the bisque, but he patched them before glazing with a kiln cement using magnesium silicate as a bonding agent. The derby was bisque-fired immediately after the stool, and the two major sections were done. All that remained were the glasses and pool balls.

The cactus frame of the eyeglasses was first done as a tube form (the method Middlebrook used on the legs of the stool) and bent and

joined into a circular shape. But this, coupled with shrinking, proved to be too much pressure on the clay and it cracked in many places. So he made the frame in the same way he did the seat, a hump-mold affair, and then cut the center out and tucked the sides around. He had to fill in the final inch with slabs of cactus-textured clay in order to complete the shape as a closed tube. This worked perfectly.

The pool rack was done with straight slab pieces attached to two corner curves he spent a lot of time forming with knives and a Surform tool. He scored and slipped two sides of the rack and slid them into the openings left for them in the cactus frame. Middlebrook then set up the bisqued stool with the bisqued hat on it and positioned the still-wet glasses the way he wanted it to look. He was determining where he needed to put a hole, so that in the final assembly, after everything was fired, a rod projecting from the stool and hat would support the eyeglasses. He decided on one side of the pool rack and worked a hole into the cactus frame. A small piece of cactus clay was then fabricated so it could be glued over the rod and hide it in the final assembly. The glasses frame was then waxed to slow down the drying.

Working from a model, Middlebrook cut two identical shapes of an oversized temple for a pair of oversized glasses. He laid each modified J-shape on a bag of vermiculite and ran his thumb and then a metal rib down the middle of each. This resulted in two bulging sections that when stuck together would have a nicely rounded contour instead of a

flat one. Before sticking the slabs together, though, he cut out about seven lemon-shaped discs that he attached down the length of one of the slabs. These ribs would keep the two halves from losing their shape. A hole cut into each disc assured there would be no air trapped in the chambers between the discs.

He then made a trip to the local hardware store and bought several hinges. When he returned to the studio, he ground the square corners of one of the hinges into rounded ones. He put the glasses frame on the table and had an assistant hold the temple piece to the pool rack. Taking into account the shrinkage that would occur during firing, he then traced the outline of the hinge on both the temple and the rack where it would finally be attached. With a dentist's pick he scraped the clay inside the outline he had made so the hinge would sit flush with the rest of the temple and the rack. He cut holes in the clay where the hinge would be attached. Both pieces were then ready to be bisqued. Because of their long shape it was impossible to lay them flat on a kiln shelf, so he leaned them against the brick part of the kiln, not an electrical element, and fired them to cone 02.

By this time, Middlebrook had decided he wanted a paintbrush in the pool rack, so he made a mold of one and took a cast of it. All that remained were the pool balls. He tried making a plaster mold of a real pool ball, but the fired casting shrank so much it didn't look like the real thing. So he went to a toy store and found a rubber ball that would

give a cast that would shrink to the right size. Both the brush and pool-ball molds were simple two-piece molds. Six pool balls were made and bisqued along with the paintbrush.

All the components were now bisqued and ready to glaze. After three weeks of fabrication, Middlebrook was eager to do some glazing but first talked about his approach to it. He said he was really not interested in the intense, bright, glassy surfaces that most low-fire pieces are done in. Yet he loves color and has figured out a technique that gives subtle and warm colors without using gloss glazes. He does depend on commercial glazes, and has the same complaints about them as most craftsmen: 1) many colors and glazes get discontinued just after you've figured out how to use them, and 2) you usually can't get what you want in bulk so it is very expensive to glaze a large piece.

Middlebrook buys color sample charts from several glaze manufacturers to determine what he wants for the piece he's working on. His glaze process is fairly complex and depends on several layers of glazes and underglazes to get the texture and color he's after. To help make the transition from white clay to layers of glaze, he usually washes the pieces with either iron oxide or manganese dioxide. He used iron on the stool and manganese on the derby. The oxide is mixed with water, brushed on, and sponged off.

On the cactus part of the stool, Middlebrook brushed on cone 05 glazes that would be seen only through the cracks that would develop through the thick layer he would apply over these glazes. He used black, brown, white, reds, and oranges, all matte glazes. Most got two coats, while the reds and oranges needed three. Some of the glaze was sponged off to give different tones and to help blend the glazes into one another.

Over these glazes he laid a thick coat of a glaze called beige bark, which provides a lot of texture for his glaze technique and provides a good surface for airbrushed underglazes. He used a mixture of 60 percent ball clay and 40 percent matte-white cone 05 glaze sprayed over the beige bark to provide a surface for the underglazes that would bring out their colors without having to use glossy transparent glazes over them. When the 60/40 mixture dried, he airbrushed on the underglaze colors. These provide the major surface color, but everything that had

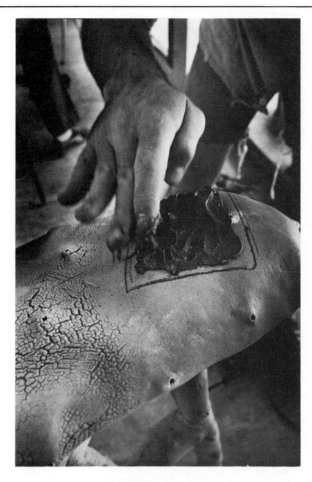

been put on underneath them contributes depth, texture, and some color to the fired piece.

On the "wood" sections of the stool and eyeglass frame, only the 60/40 mixture was used before the underglazes were put on, so the texture of the wood grain in the clay wouldn't be destroyed. It also provides a nice contrast to the juicier color and texture of the cactus parts. The derby was also glazed just with the 60/40 mixture and a gray underglaze. The temple was given a mock tortoiseshell finish by brushing brown and black underglazes on and wiping them off at an angle. It was then covered with a thin coat of a clear satin glaze.

The pool balls were glazed in brilliant gloss glazes with hand-painted numbers. The 10 ball was given a splash of mauve glaze that was also used on the hairs of the paintbrush. (The 10 ball and paintbrush were joined together during the final assembly.)

Each piece was given just one firing at cone 05, though it took three separate firings to get all the pieces done using just the one kiln.

When all the pieces were fired, Middlebrook got out his drills, rods, and epoxy. With a masonry bit he drilled a 1/4-inch hole in the seat of the stool. The hole was drilled at the same angle as one of the legs of the stool so that a rod stuck in the hole would go down the hollow leg. Another hole was drilled in the depression in the hat, at the same angle, and one more through a block of wood that was epoxied to the seat of the stool. A 1/4-inch steel rod was then passed through the wood and seat and pushed all the way down the leg. The hat was then set over the rod and onto the seat of the stool. The pool-ball rack was set into the depression in the hat and the rod run up the side of the rack into the cactus portion of the frame. The little cactus coverlet was then epoxied into place to hide the rod.

The temple piece was drilled to receive the holding end of the paintbrush. The temple was then hinged to the eyeframe. The pool balls were epoxied into position in and on the rack. Lastly the paintbrush was epoxied to the 10 ball and slipped into the hole in the temple at the other end. Although the piece was now complete, it could still be broken down into four sections for shipping. For a view of the finished project see color Plate 15.

Plate 1. Ralph Bacerra. Covered jar. 17″ diameter. An outline drawing of the design was done on porcelain bisque with a brush dipped in a mixture of cobalt and water. The piece was then glazed and fired to cone 10. China paints were hand-painted over the fired glaze and the piece was then fired to cone 018. *(Photograph by Ralph Bacerra)*

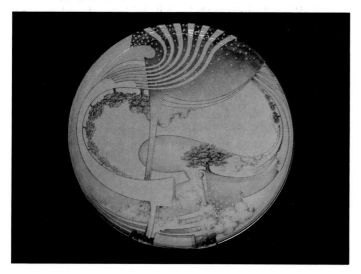

Plate 2. Al Widenhofer. "Tornado Deco." 22″ diameter. Underglaze pencil drawn on bisqued white clay and hardened on by firing to cone 06. A clear glaze was thinly airbrushed over drawing and then also fired to cone 06. Some of the pencil lines were darkened by brushing them lightly immediately after application with water. The plate is highlighted by platinum luster. *(Photograph by Al Widenhofer)*

Plate 3. Patti Warashina. "You Captured My Heart." 30″ high. Constructed from slab and cast pieces of white clay. Drawing was done by airbrushing underglazes onto bisqued piece. These were then set by firing to cone 05 with *no glazes* used over them. After firing, the piece was sprayed with acrylic fixative. *(Photograph by Patti Warashina)*

Plate 4. Patti Warashina. "Midnight Masquerade." 30″ high. Same technique as Plate 3. *(Photograph by Patti Warashina)*

Plate 5. Nancy Carman. "Making Up for Lost Time." 7¹/₂″ by 10″ by 24″. Fabricated from slabs and coils of white clay. Decorated with underglaze pencils, underglazes, glazes, and china paints. *(Photograph by Nancy Carman)*

Plate 6. Nancy Carman. "Self-Portrait." 7¹/₂″ by 16¹/₂″ by 16″. Made from white clay slabs. Finished with underglaze pencils, underglazes, glazes, and china paints. *(Photograph by Nancy Carman)*

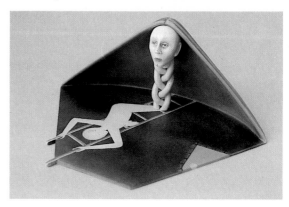

Plate 7. Joe Bova. "Pork Sword" (detail). 14″ by 9¹/₂″ by 23″. Sculpted from slabs draped over stuffed bags and from extruded and thrown parts. China paints applied by brush to unglazed bisque and fired to cone 018. *(Photograph by Joe Bova)*

Plate 8. Will Herrera. "Bird of Paradise." 32″ tall. See pages 15–25. *(Photograph by David Powers)*

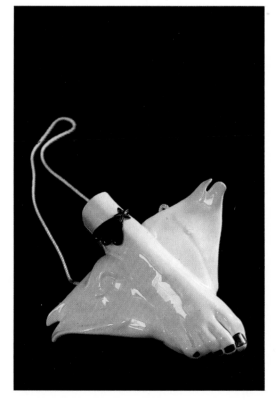

Plate 9. Will Herrera. Winged-foot planter. 5″ by 9″ by 10″. A cast starburst was attached to the cast winged foot. Platinum luster was used on the star and toenails to finish the piece. *(Photograph by David Powers)*

Plate 10. Ron Nagle. Cup. 4$^{1}/_{2}$″ by 3$^{1}/_{2}$″. Constructed from thin slabs of clay, this cup gets its rich colors from as many as 15 successive china paint applications and firings. *(Photograph courtesy of Quay Ceramics Gallery)*

Plate 11. David Furman. "Molly on a Pink Couch." 12″ by 12″. *(Photograph courtesy of Quay Ceramics Gallery)*

Plate 12. Mineo Mizuno. Cups. 5″ by 6″. These cups were assembled from slab and wheel-thrown pieces and finished with cone 04 glazes. *(Photograph by David Powers)*

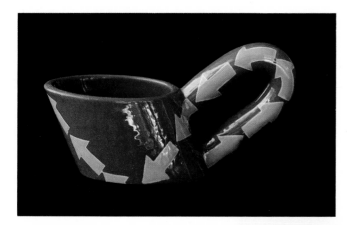

Plate 13. Mineo Mizuno. Cup 6″ by 4″. *(Photograph by David Powers)*

Plate 14. Mineo Mizuno. Untitled. 21″ tall. Constructed from slabs and wheel-thrown pieces, this giant screw was finished with cone 04 glazes. *(Photograph by David Powers)*

Plate 16. David Middlebrook. "Pressure Cookin'." 46″ tall. See pages 60–73. For glaze technique on the rings see page 89. *(Photograph courtesy of Forest Jones)*

Plate 15. David Middlebrook. "Big-Game Hunter." 52″ tall. See pages 60–73. *(Photograph by David Powers)*

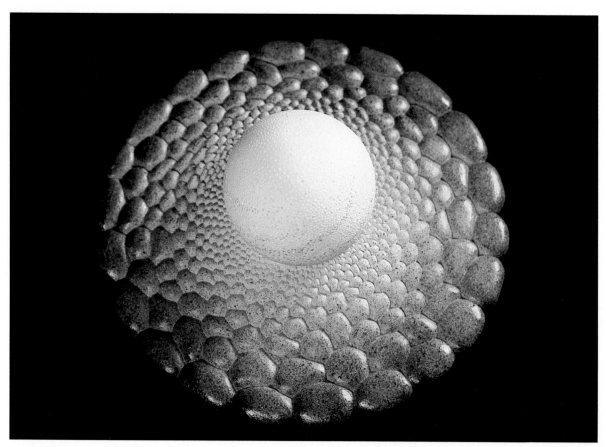

Plate 17. Duane Ewing. "A.R.T. Dome." 12″ diameter. See pages 107–115. *(Photograph by David Powers)*

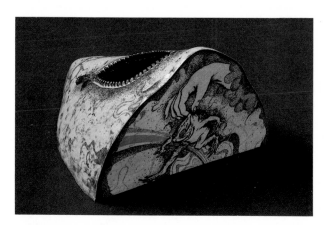

Plate 18. Duane Ewing. "The Casting Out of the Gilhooligans from the Kingdom of Heaven." 9″ by 10″ by 8″. This piece was handbuilt from slabs. The drawing was done with underglaze pencil on bisque. Brushed and dotted underglazes were used to finish the design. After a hardening-on firing, a clear glaze was applied and fired to cone 05. Gold luster was then used on the zipper. *(Photograph by David Powers)*

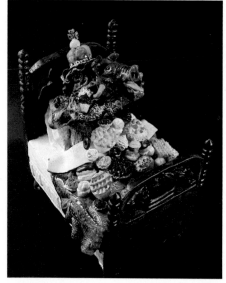

Plate 19. David Gilhooley. "Victoria's Royal Snack." 16$\frac{1}{2}$″ by 9$\frac{1}{2}$″ by 11$\frac{1}{2}$″. *(Photograph courtesy of Hansen Fuller Gallery)*

Plate 20. Karen Breschi. "Cat Mother." 10″ by 11³/₄″. Bisqued clay painted with acrylics. *(Photograph courtesy of Quay Ceramics Gallery)*

Plate 21. Chris Unterseher. "Bobby Koefer." 23″ by 9″. *(Photograph courtesy of Quay Ceramics Gallery)*

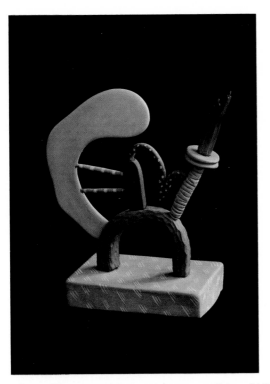

Plate 23. Tom Rippon. Necklace and pins. Same technique as Plate 22. *(Photograph courtesy of Quay Ceramics Gallery)*

Plate 22. Tom Rippon. Untitled. 8″ by 9¹/₂″. The colors in this piece come from luster glazes applied and fired over *unglazed* bisque clay. *(Photograph courtesy of Quay Ceramics Gallery)*

Plate 24. Karen Clausen and Susan Hollenbeck. Pins. Each pin 1¹/₄″ diameter. All these pins were hand-formed. *(Photograph by David Powers)*

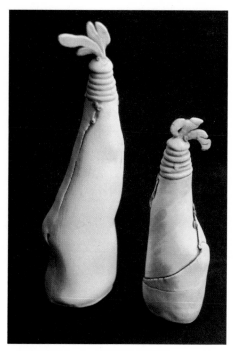

Plate 25. Claudia Tarantino. Miniature covered jars. 3″ and 4″ tall. Thin slabs and coils make up these delicate pieces. *(Photograph by David Powers)*

Plate 26. Edward Bear. "Mercenary." 12″ tall. This was handbuilt from red earthenware clay while the claws, teeth and eyes were done with white clay. The piece was highlighted by the use of oxides brushed on and then sponged off bisque before the final firing. *(Photograph by David Powers)*

Plate 27. John Roloff. Untitled. 29½″ long. Handbuilt and unglazed. *(Photograph courtesy of John Jones)*

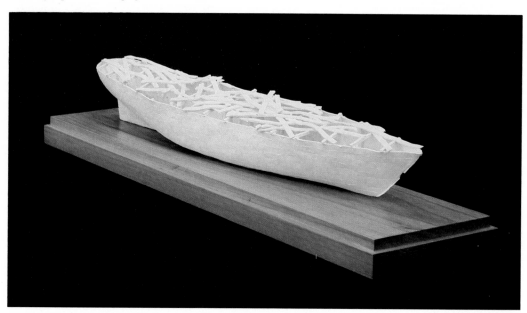

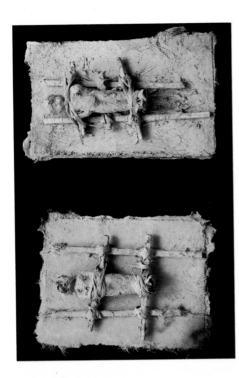

Plate 28. John Bobeda. "Relics." 8″ by 8″ and 7″ by 9″. These were made with white clay slabs laminated together with slip and fiberglass cloth. *(Photograph by David Powers)*

Plate 29. John Bobeda. "Kite Fragment." 2′ by 3′. See pages 55–56. *(Photograph by David Powers)*

Plate 30. Dan Oberti. Untitled. 18″ tall. See page 123. *(Photograph by David Powers)*

Plate 31. Harvey Brody. "Shrine to the Mad Dog." 7″ by 7¹/₂″ by 11″. Constructed from slabs and finished with underglazes, glaze, and platinum luster. *(Photograph by David Powers)*

Plate 32. Harvey Brody. "Altered Piece #1." 12″ tall. This piece was fabricated from slabs and coils. *(Photographed by David Powers)*

Plate 33. Richard Moquin. Covered jars. 14″ tall. These pieces were thrown on a wheel. Slab letters have been added to their tops. *(Photograph courtesy of Meyer Breier Weiss Gallery)*

Plate 34. Bill Abright. "Erecto-pyre." 20″ by 14″. Wheel-thrown plate had two of its sides cut. Sticks comprising the pyre were extruded, fired separately, and then assembled in the fired plate. All pieces were raku fired. *(Photograph by David Powers)*

Plate 35. Bill Abright. "Harvey's Bird." See pages 125–135. *(Photograph by David Powers)*

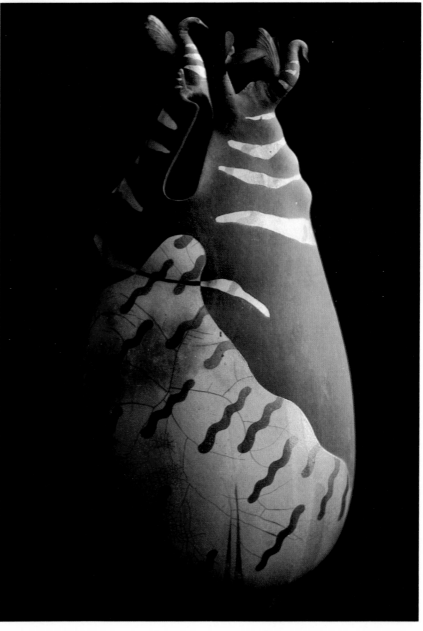

Plate 36. Robert Hudson. "Untitled Ceramic #38." 13¹/₂″ by 11¹/₄″ by 7¹/₂″. Constructed from cast pieces assembled in leather-hard state. Colors are from underglazes and china paints. *(Photograph courtesy of Hansen Fuller Gallery)*

Plate 37. Robert Hudson. "#11 Jar." 16¹/₂″ by 10″ by 7¹/₂″. Assembled from cast pieces and decorated entirely with underglazes brushed and airbrushed on bisque. *(Photograph courtesy of John Jones)*

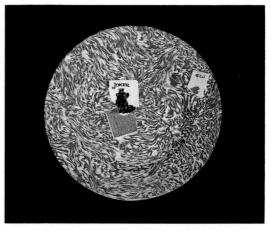

Plate 39. Richard Shaw. Marbled plate with decals. 18″ in diameter. See pages 40–49. *(Photograph by David Powers)*

Plate 38. Richard Shaw. Teapot. 6″ by 12″. Cast pieces were assembled to produce this "teapot." Underglazes and china paints on bisque provide shading and color. *(Photograph by David Powers)*

Plate 40. Richard Shaw. Plate with decals. 18″ in diameter. See pages 40–49. *(Photograph by David Powers)*

How Low Can You Go?: Low-Fire Glazes

On Your Way Down

Imagine ceramics as a constant journey. We've just taken an enjoyable train ride through the fascinating Land of Clay and have now arrived at the vast Ocean of Glazes, where we'll set sail and discover that some of us get seasick.

Glazing *is* a different way of working; glazes do not have the tactile, substantive qualities of clay. They form a liquid, surface world that goes *on top of* the clay. Glazing is also quite mysterious and elusive, since it doesn't always work the way you might expect. The clay puts your eyes and hands into instant agreement; form and texture remain within your immediate control while the clay is still plastic. The color of clay may change during firing, but this is minimal compared to the change in most glazes. The wait between application of the glaze and the finished firing and cooling often drives people mad with anticipation. I've cracked lots of pieces by opening kilns too soon because I just had to see what the pieces looked like. But my curiosity isn't all that difficult to understand, considering the spectacular colors possible with low-fire glazes.

You can deal with glazing on various levels, although many artists choose not to deal with it at all—leaving the clay to do all the surface expression. In John Bobeda's kite form

(Plate 29) and John Roloff's piece (Plate 27), the forms and details are so strong they need no glazes. Will Herrera's "Winged Foot" (Plate 9) uses a single glaze that adds another surface dimension to the clay without disturbing its form.

You can utilize the chemistry involved in the preparation of glazes to make your own or totally ignore it and work comfortably out of jars and tubes of materials made commercially. Some of the processes and techniques of low-fire glazing are time-consuming enough without having to spend more time making glazes. There are so many glazes on the market that the biggest problem you might have is being able to test them all. (This easy availability indicates that much of the preparation isn't all that difficult.)

This chapter concentrates on glaze processes and techniques, rather than formal chemical analyses. Enough basic glaze chemistry is presented, however, to allow an uncomplicated understanding of how glazes are made and how and why they work. The person who wants more complete technical information should read Daniel Rhodes's *Clay and Glazes for the Potter* or Cullen Parmalee and Cameron Harman's *Ceramic Glazes*.

Looking into Glazes

Glazes are surface coatings used to seal and decorate clay. They are made of very finely ground materials and mixed with water or oils and binders so they can be easily applied to clay surfaces. The bond between the clay and the glaze is made permanent by heating the two in a kiln so the glaze *melts* and *adheres* to the clay. Chemically, glazes are very closely related to glass.

Flux-Alumina-Silica

Silica is the basis for almost all glass and glaze formulation. When heated to its melting point and cooled quickly, it produces clear glass. Because of silica's high melting point (over 1700°C), low-fire glazes and most commercial glass use *fluxes* to lower the melting point to a workable range. Molten glass needs to flow easily in order to be rolled into windows or cast or blown into bottles. Glazes, on the other hand, usually need a higher viscosity so they won't flow off the clay when fired. A stiffening agent, usually *alumina*, Al_2O_3, is used to make the molten glaze flow like maple syrup, compared to the watery flow of molten glass. Alumina also helps prevent crystals from forming as the glaze cools. This is why most *crystalline glazes*, which are low in alumina, tend to run so much.

Glazes, then, are made up of three basic components: silica, fluxes, and alumina. With a range of fluxes to choose from, each giving different results, and by varying the proportions of silica, flux, and alumina, an unending parade of glazes can march through your kilns. In glaze formulation, it is common practice to refer to the three glaze components by a kind of chemical shorthand: RO for most fluxes, R_2O_3 for alumina, and RO_2 for silica. *O* is the chemical notation for *oxygen* and *R* is any earth element that combines with oxygen in some specific ratio, indicated by the subscript numbers. Thus alumina, Al_2O_3, is categorized (with some other compounds) under the general heading R_2O_3. For our purposes, however, I will continue to use the generic names of these substances.

Fluxes generally used in low-fire glazes are:

PbO	Lead Oxide
MgO	Magnesium Oxide
BaO	Barium Oxide
CaO	Calcium Oxide
SrO	Strontium Oxide
ZnO	Zinc Oxide
Li_2O	Lithium Oxide
Na_2O	Sodium Oxide
K_2O	Potassium Oxide
B_2O_3	Boric Oxide

Boric oxide, B_2O_3, is grouped in the alumina-R_2O_3 group when determining formulas, as are iron oxide, Fe_2O_3, antimony oxide, Sb_2O_3, and chromium oxide, Cr_2O_3. Silica, SiO_2, then, takes up the last group of glass formers, the RO_2 group, along with titanium oxide, TiO_2, and zirconium oxide, ZrO_2.

Organizing the oxides involved in glaze formulation into these groups helps clarify the component parts of a glaze and will help simplify glaze calculations should you choose to do them.

It would be very tidy and efficient if all the oxides involved in glaze formulation were readily and cheaply available in their simple states. Calculations would be a snap. But Nature provides in her own sweet way, often dishing up raw materials that have complicated mixtures of more than one oxide in them, other materials that are soluble, and some that are toxic. Man, the chemist, however, strikes back as far as solubility and toxicity are concerned.

You'll remember from our discussion in chapter 1 that *frits* are compounds made to render certain chemicals like lead and boron more usable. There are hundreds of commercial frits, and they make up a large source of oxides for glazes. Not only does fritting lessen or eliminate solubility and toxicity, but it also helps to remove some gases before the chemicals are put on a clay surface. This can eliminate pinholing and blistering caused by gases boiling through the glaze surface.

Since frits are so helpful, you should always try to use them when you make glazes. But if you have to use soluble materials, these are the things you should know and do:

1. Since soluble materials will dissolve in the water that is used to mix the glaze, don't ever throw any of the water out, and try to keep it from evaporating by storing the glazes in tightly covered jars.

2. When such a glaze is applied to a clay surface, the clay absorbs some of the water with the dissolved material, thus altering the glaze composition by depriving it of some of the soluble material and changing the clay composition by adding the solubles to it. Therefore, apply glazes that have soluble materials in them to semivitreous ware, which won't absorb any of the water.

3. Some of the solubles are caustic, so you need to handle them carefully and wear rubber gloves. This is especially true of pearl ash and soda ash.

These are the more common soluble materials used in low-fire glazes:

Boric Acid

Borax

Pearl Ash

Soda Ash

Fluxes and Their Sources

Lead Oxide

We are all aware of the toxic nature of raw lead, and the possible toxicity that can result from its improper use in fired glazes. A little paranoia is sound policy in dealing with such a useful but deadly material. However, there is no need to avoid lead completely, since it does add some unique properties to glazes and is widely available in fritted forms, which considerably reduce the risk involved in using it. Read carefully "Poisons in the Glazeroom" on page 84.

Lead is a cheap source of a very strong flux, and generally produces bright, smooth glazes. It has a low coefficient of expansion, which means there is little problem getting a lead glaze to fit a clay body. (See "Fits and Faults," page 87.) Lead glazes usually have a wide firing range, often more than 5 cones, so you can get good results at, for example, cone 06, 05, 04, 03, 02, 01, and cone 1 with the same lead glaze. Some drawbacks of lead, other than its toxicity, are that it generally produces soft glaze surfaces, which are easily scratched, and that it reduces easily, which can cause it to blister or turn gray or black if flame or smoke come in contact with it. This can be avoided, of course, by firing in an electric kiln or by doing careful oxidation firings in a gas kiln (see page 90).

Sources

Litharge, PbO

White Lead, Lead Carbonate, $2PbCO_3 \cdot Pb(OH)_2$

Red Lead, Pb_3O_4

Lead Silicates: these are the fritted and safer forms of lead and should be used whenever possible; fritting lead with silica makes the lead much less soluble and, therefore, much less toxic. Fritted lead is also much less susceptible to reduction than raw lead.

Lead Monosilicate:	84% PbO
	16% SiO_2
Lead Bisilicate:	65% PbO
	33% SiO_2
	2% Al_2O_3

Magnesium Oxide

In low-fire glazes, magnesium oxide (MgO) doesn't have much fluxing power and acts more as a refractory material, creating matteness and opacity in glazes.

Sources

Magnesium Carbonate, $MgCO_3$

Dolomite, $CaCO_3 \cdot MgCO_3$

Talc, $3MgO \cdot 4SiO_2 \cdot H_2O$

Barium Oxide

Barium oxide (BaO) is another refractory in low-fire, and can be used in small amounts to produce matte surfaces in glazes.

Source

Barium Carbonate, $BaCO_3$ (poisonous)

Calcium Oxide

Calcium (CaO) is a good addition to low-fire glazes, but must be used in conjunction with other fluxes to cause glaze melting. It increases the hardness of fired glazes and also reduces the coefficient of expansion, making it easier to fit the glaze to a clay body.

Sources

Whiting, Calcium Carbonate, $CaCO_3$. This is the most common and cheapest source of calcium for glaze purposes.

Dolomite, $CaCO_3 \cdot MgCO_3$

CaO is found in most feldspars and many frits.

Colemanite or Gerstley Borate, $2CaO \cdot 3B_2O_3 \cdot 5H_2O$

Bone Ash, $Ca_3(PO_4)_2$

Wollastonite, $CaSiO_3$

Fluorspar, CaF_2. This is rarely used in glazes because it causes bubbling, though it is a powerful flux.

Zinc Oxide

In small amounts, zinc oxide (ZnO) can help smooth out glazes, but in larger amounts—i.e., as a primary flux—it will cause crawling since it is really not strong enough to use as a primary flux in low-fire glazes. It also affects coloring oxides in the glaze: iron and zinc will produce muddy colors, copper and zinc give brilliant blues and greens, and zinc with chrome inhibits green.

Source

Zinc Oxide, ZnO

Strontium Oxide

Strontium oxide (SrO) affects glazes very much like calcium, except that it is a slightly stronger flux. Because it is so expensive, though, it is rarely used.

Source

Strontium Carbonate, $SrCO_3$

Lithium Oxide

Lithium oxide (Li_2O) has a low coefficient of expansion, which helps to prevent crazing in glazes and to give a good fit to a clay body. It is an active but expensive flux.

Sources

Lepidolite, $LiF \cdot KF \cdot Al_2O_3 \cdot 3SiO_2$

Spodumene, $Li_2O \cdot Al_2O_3 \cdot 4SiO_2$

Lithium Carbonate, Li_2CO_3

Petalite, $Li_2O \cdot Al_2O_3 \cdot 8SiO_2$

Amblygonite, $2LiF \cdot Al_2O_3 \cdot P_2O_5$

Sodium Oxide

Sodium oxide (Na_2O) is a very strong and active flux that gives good brilliant colors with coloring oxides. It has a high coefficient of expansion, so that glazes high in sodium will generally craze on clay bodies. High-soda glazes have soft, scratchable surfaces.

Sources

Soda Ash, Na_2CO_3 (soluble)

Borax, $Na_2O \cdot 2B_2O_3 \cdot 10H_2O$ (soluble)

Soda feldspars and frits

Nepheline Syenite, $K_2O \cdot 3Na_2O \cdot 4Al_2O_3 \cdot 9SiO_2$

Cryolite, Na_3AlF_6. The flourine in cryolite can cause bubbling problems in glazes, leading to cratered and pinholed fired surfaces.

Potassium Oxide

Potassium oxide (K_2O) may yield even more brilliant colors than sodium when used with colorants. It also increases the surface hardness in glazes while decreasing the coefficient of expansion.

Sources

Nepheline Syenite, $K_2O \cdot 3Na_2O \cdot 4Al_2O_3 \cdot 9SiO_2$

Potash feldspars and frits

Pearl Ash, K_2CO_3 (soluble)

Boric Oxide

Boric oxide (B_2O_3) has strong fluxing properties, like lead, and has a low coefficient of expansion. Like sodium and potassium, boric oxide can give brilliant colors.

Sources

Colemanite or Gerstley Borate, $2CaO \cdot 3B_2O_3 \cdot 5H_2O$

Frits

Boric Acid, $B_2O_3 \cdot 2H_2O$ (soluble)

Borax, $Na_2O \cdot 2B_2O_3 \cdot 10H_2O$ (soluble)

Alumina and Its Sources

Alumina (Al_2OR_3) is a major component of naturally occurring clays and feldspars. In glazes it acts as a stiffening agent to help prevent a molten glaze from flowing off a clay body when fired.

Sources

Feldspars

Frits

Clay, $Al_2O_3 \cdot 2SiO_2 \cdot 2H_2O$. Clay is important in glaze formulation, as it helps keep other materials in suspension and "glue" them to the clay body before firing.

Pyrophyllite, $Al_2O_3 \cdot 4SiO_2 \cdot H_2O$

Silica and Its Sources

Silica (SiO_2) is an abundant material that is the basis of all glazes.

Sources

Silica or Flint, SiO_2

Feldspars

Frits

Clay, $Al_2O_3 \cdot 2SiO_2 \cdot 2H_2O$

Pyrophyllite, $Al_2O_3 \cdot 4SiO_2 \cdot H_2O$

Talc, $3MgO \cdot 4SiO_2 \cdot H_2O$

Nepheline Syenite,
$K_2O \cdot 3Na_2O \cdot 4Al_2O_3 \cdot 9SiO_2$

Lepidolite, $LiF \cdot KF \cdot Al_2O_3 \cdot 3SiO_2$

Spodumene, $Li_2O \cdot Al_2O_3 \cdot 4SiO_2$

Petalite, $Li_2O \cdot Al_2O_3 \cdot 8SiO_2$

The flux-alumina-silica system is an easy guide to the theory of glazes and how they work. It also determines which raw materials get used in the actual making of glazes. Because of this relationship, glazes can be expressed in two different forms.

Two Ways of Mixing Glazes

The Empirical Formula reduces glazes to their active ingredients of flux-alumina-silica and denotes them in molecular proportions. This is what a cone 06 lead glaze looks like:

Flux		Alumina		Silica	
PbO	.65	Al_2O_3	.20	SiO_2	1.20
K_2O	.15				
CaO	.20				

By convention, everything in the flux column is made to add up to one. So in this formula, we know at a glance that for every 65 molecules of lead oxide, PbO, there are 15 molecules of potassium oxide, K_2O, 20 molecules of calcium oxide, CaO, 20 molecules of alumina, Al_2O_3, and 120 molecules of silica, SiO_2. If you would like to learn the system chemists have devised so they don't have to pick and sort molecules all day in order to put a glaze to-gether, you can do so in either of the two books recommended at the beginning of this chapter. It is useful for anyone involved in his or her own glazes to be able to do this, for often you'll run across glazes written in this form, or perhaps a glaze recipe you have will call for a raw material you can't get and for which you'll therefore need to find a replacement. But for the most part these are minor considerations for most ceramicists. However, as you will see in the sections discussing glaze, underglaze, and overglaze colorants, the flux-alumina-silica components of any glaze greatly affect *fired colors*, so you should familiarize yourself with the raw materials and be able to tell what their active ingredients are.

The Batch Recipe lists the raw materials and their proportions by weight. This is the form you'll usually find glazes written in. Here is a cone 06 glaze recipe that contains lithium and boron fluxes:

Spodumene	21.3
Colemanite	65.5
Kaolin	12.1
Silica	1.1
	100.0

for dark blue add 1 percent cobalt carbonate

The numbers refer to parts-by-weight of the raw materials regardless of what weight system is used: pounds, grams, tons, etc. So for 100 pounds of dry glaze, you'd need 21.3 pounds of spodumene, 65.5 pounds of colemanite, 12.1 pounds of kaolin, and 1.1 pounds of silica. This is what's known as a *base glaze*, because it has no colorants in it. Colorants and stains are usually added as percentages of the dry weight of the base glaze. Here, for example, a 1 percent addition of cobalt carbonate means adding 1 pound of cobalt to the 100 pounds of base glaze.

I want to note here that glaze-making historically has been a trial-and-error process, throwing a little of this and a little of that together and *seeing* what happens. You can still work this way, intuitively, more easily in low-fire than in high-fire, since most of the commercial frits themselves will make fine glazes at cone 06. With a little ball clay (5 to 15 percent) added to them, they will adhere to your clay pieces. When there are *particular* results you want from a glaze, however, you may not want to spend twenty years experimenting, especially when it's possible for you to produce those results in one hour simply because other people put in those years of experimentation. The last word, though, is this: regardless of theory and someone else's experience, fired glaze results are subject to so many variables that although there are predictable results, nothing is certain until you see what comes out of your kiln. That should put an edge on things for you.

The list of raw materials and sources for the fluxes, alumina, and silica used in low-fire glazes is small enough to be comfortably mastered, yet can be varied and mixed in so many ways as to provide for an infinite number of possible glazes. Glazes are much less complicated to make than, say, underglazes and overglazes, so you can become somewhat independent of commercial preparations if you choose.

Other Considerations

In our quick run-through on glazes so far, the flux-alumina-silica system provides a base glaze whose *texture* and *color* are undetermined. In comparing glaze with glass, I planted the image of clear, transparent glaze that would allow you to see through to the clay body it covered. But sometimes it just ain't so. Many of the materials that make up glazes can cloud them up. This is particularly true in low-fire glazes high in boric oxide, which not only get milky but take on a bluish cast. A glaze high in alumina, zinc, or barium may also get cloudy. If *opacity* is what you want in a glaze, then the surest way to get it is by adding materials that are not easily melted by the glaze but remain suspended in it. These

are called *opacifiers*. *Tin oxide*, SnO_2, is by far the strongest opacifier. A base glaze requires about 5 percent tin to make it completely opaque white. Tin, however, is very expensive, which has led to the use of other opacifiers.

Titanium oxide, TiO_2, in amounts up to 12 percent of a glaze will opacify it. *Zirconium oxide*, ZrO_2, is generally used in a fritted form (*opax* and *zircopax* are the most common brand names). This, too, needs to be used in amounts up to 12 percent of a glaze in order to make it opaque white.

Making a clear glaze opaque also dulls its surface so that it no longer reflects light as brilliantly. If a glaze's surface is still smooth but has no shine or "glassiness" it is termed a *matte* (or mat) finish. This can be produced by adding alumina or barium carbonate to an otherwise glossy low-fire glaze. If the glaze becomes rough to the touch it is *underfired*. Underfired glazes that produce rough surfaces can be very effective for some work, but should not be used on surfaces that come in contact with food or drink, particularly if there is lead in the glaze.

You'll recall from our discussion in chapter 1 that there are several metallic oxides and prepared stains that are used to color clay bodies. Glazes are colored in the same way, by adding oxides and stains. Because glazes are a much more suitable and therefore important medium for developing subtle colors, glaze color is an extensive field of study, often yielding exotic and expensive materials. These not only function in glazes, they also form the bases for *underglazes* and *overglazes*. (See pages 89 and 93.)

Now it must be understood that while an oxide or stain causes *some* color to appear in glazes, the *other components* of the glaze— i.e. flux-alumina-silica—have an effect on what the particular color will be. This is especially true of the fluxes. Since different fluxes also impart certain characteristics such as hardness and brilliancy to the glaze itself, low-fire glazes are usually classified by the major flux in them: lead, boron, or alkaline (see pages 77–79).

Colors

Blues are achieved with *cobalt oxide*, Co_2O_3, or *cobalt carbonate*, $CoCO_3$. Both are very strong and can give a range of blues when used from 0.25 to 2 percent. Blues can be modified with *nickel oxide, iron oxide*, or *manganese oxide* used in small (1 to 2 percent) amounts. Leadless glazes using cobalt tend to produce colder blues than do lead glazes. Turquoise-blue glazes are gotten in highly alkaline glazes with the addition of 3 to 5 percent *copper oxide* and 5 to 10 percent *tin oxide*.

Greens in lead glazes are achieved with *copper oxide* used in amounts varying from 1 to 5 percent. But copper in lead glazes makes lead more soluble and therefore a potent source of lead poisoning when used for food and drink containers. *Nickel oxide* used in glazes containing magnesium oxide will produce greens in lead or leadless glazes; use between 2 and 5 percent. *Chromium oxide*, usually gotten from *potassium dichromate*, $K_2Cr_2O_7$, will give green glazes, but will go brown in the presence of zinc oxide, pink in the presence of tin oxides.

Yellows have several sources. *Molybdenum oxide* in amounts from 2 to 10 percent in lead glazes will produce yellow. Then there are several yellow stains that work in either lead or leadless glazes: *tin-vanadium* stain, from 4 to 6 percent; *zirconium-vanadium* stain, from 5 to 10 percent; *lead-antimony* stain, from 3 to 5 percent; and *praseodymium* stain, from 4 to 6 percent.

Oranges, the earthier oranges, come from *chrome-alumina* stain and *chrome-iron-zinc* stain. Bright oranges are produced in lead glazes by *cadmium-selenium* stain.

Reds are obtained in lead glazes with *chrome-tin* stains used in amounts of about 5 percent. These stains will give colors ranging from red to pink. Some muted reds are produced with *iron oxide* in alkaline glazes with high silica content; use from 3 to 5 percent iron. Rose colors are achieved in alkaline glazes by adding 0.1 percent *gold chloride*.

Browns and tans can be achieved with *iron oxide*—either red, Fe_2O_3, or black, Fe_3O_4—when added to a glaze in amounts from 2 to 5 percent. Alkaline glazes produce cooler brown colors than lead glazes. *Manganese oxide* will also produce browns and tans in lead or leadless glazes; use from 1 to 8 percent. *Chromium oxide* will give light browns and tans when used in lead glazes containing zinc.

Blacks need an overload of colorants. An addition of 1 percent *cobalt oxide*, from 6 to 9 percent *iron oxide*, and from 2 to 4 percent *manganese oxide*, will give black. *Black stain*, used from 4 to 8 percent in any glaze, will produce black.

Rewind and Mix

Getting a glaze together requires mixing all the components that we've discussed:

1. Flux

2. Alumina

3. Silica

4. Opacifying agent if opacity is desired

5. Metallic oxide or stain if color is desired

And to complete the list

6. Additives.

Certain raw materials, especially feldspars and colemanite, sink to the bottom of a wet mixed glaze and harden there. This makes it difficult to remix and difficult to maintain the same glaze composition. Generally, if a glaze has clay in it (ball clay, kaolin, etc.) its ingredients won't settle too badly. If there isn't enough clay, or if the glaze is a real sinker, 1 to 3 percent *bentonite* can be added.

Another problem, particularly for low-fire glazes, is making sure the glaze will *adhere* to the clay body when applied. As mentioned, many of the commercial frits alone make suitable glazes at cone 06, but need some ball clay added to them in order to stick to a piece of clay. So again, clay and bentonite can help a glaze, ensuring its adherence to a clay body.

Methocel is a binder which also helps keep glazes in suspension; it doesn't decompose the way organic binders and gums do. So if adding bentonite doesn't work, try this: Dissolve some methocel in hot water and let it soak for a day. If the result of this soaking looks like jelly, pour it into more hot water so it becomes a thick liquid; then add to the wet mixed glaze. Only 1 to 2 percent dry weight of methocel to dry weight of glaze should do it, but don't worry about being exact. Pour dissolved methocel in until you can get the glaze to adhere to your pieces. Check page 89 for hot tips on glazing vitrified clay.

Time then to get out your dust respirator and mix up some glaze. The raw materials listed as sources for the glaze components can be purchased at ceramic-supply stores. These materials are sold in small or large amounts, with appropriate savings for big purchases. However, unless you are already committed to making and using enormous amounts of glaze, buy in small quantities —5, 10, or 25 pounds for frits and other sources of flux-alumina-silica. Colorants and stains are expensive and can be bought in packages of $\frac{1}{4}$, $\frac{1}{2}$, or 1 pound.

If you are working on glaze tests—that is, any *new* glaze, whether it's a recipe you found in your basement or something that came to you in a dream—record your procedures in your notebook as you go along, so you can repeat your successes, eliminate the duds, or, perhaps, better direct those dreams.

1. On a gram or pound scale, weigh out each ingredient according to your recipe. You should be wearing your dust respirator.

2. After weighing each material, place it in a container large enough to hold the entire glaze batch.

3. You do not have to shake or mix the dry ingredients; doing so will only cause dust.

4. Add enough water to cover the dry ingredients and let it slake for ten or fifteen minutes, until all the water is absorbed by the dry ingredients. Add more water if needed to ensure that the mixture will be liquid.

5. Mix the liquid with an appropriate utensil (teaspoon, wooden spoon, wire whisk). A very useful mixing tool can be bought as an attachment for your electric drill. The same attachment used to mix slip clay can be used for large batches of glaze, but there is also a smaller tool that will handle smaller batches of glaze. At this point you will have a better idea how thick your mixture really is. Final glaze consistency can run from thick cream to milk, depending on how thick you want or need to apply it. This can be determined only from experience, but when making a new untried glaze, I always go for the consistency of half-and-half.

6. The mixed glaze is then passed twice through a 50-mesh screen in order to mix all particles of raw materials. It is important to get a homogeneous mixture. If you are doing glaze tests—in which case you need not make more than 200 grams of glaze—the mixing can be done in a jar with a tight lid by shaking it vigorously for several minutes. Unless you have some coarse material in the glaze, such as barium carbonate or zinc oxide, you need not screen the tests.

Glazes can be stored in glass bottles or plastic buckets. If they have tight lids, none of the water will evaporate when the glaze is not being used. You need to check the glaze consistency, adding water if it has gotten too thick, and thoroughly mixing the glaze again before using. How much glaze to make up is something you'll have to determine for yourself. If it's a glaze you'll be using a lot of—that is, to cover a lot of pieces—you'll probably want to make enough so you can *dip* the pieces right into the glaze bucket, which is the best way to get an even coat. Otherwise the glaze can be *poured*, *sprayed*, or *brushed* over a piece. Some glazes tend not to smooth out in the firing, so brushing often leads to streaks or drips or unevenness. If smoothness is desirable, pour, dip, or spray.

Poisons in the Glazeroom: A Not-So-Mellow Drama

When it's time to glaze your pieces, let this section and your sense of survival guide you, for there are several toxic substances commonly used in low-fire glazes, and several ways the ceramicist and his friends, pets, and customers can suffer because of them.

Lead poisoning from already-fired ware has gotten the most publicity, for, after all, it affects the public, who outnumber ceramicists and who expect to get healthier, not sicker, from drinking orange juice.

Lead is particularly insidious because the human body has no way to get rid of it once it's in the system. Consequently, after a number of years of taking in small quantities of lead, one can "all of a sudden" have lead poisoning. For the glaze enthusiast, the danger starts with the use of raw lead compounds in glazes; the contamination may come by breathing the dust while weighing and mixing glazes, breathing the mist when applying the wet glaze, or by getting lead glaze into an open cut. Individuals do have different tolerance levels—a dose that sickens one person may go unnoticed by another—but that's hardly a comforting fact, since everyone has *some* level at which he or she succumbs. (How much lead does it take to make you sick? You don't find out until you get sick.)

The advent of lead frits has certainly made fired lead glazes much safer to use, and at the same time made the handling of raw materials much safer for anyone preparing and using glazes. But to date there is no standard of toxicity for lead frits in the raw state. Let me explain: materials can only be toxic to us if they can get into our blood system, and in order for that to happen they need to be soluble in stomach acid or blood—that is, able to dissolve the way salt does in water.

Raw lead compounds are extremely soluble; however, when they are fritted and fused with silica they start to lose this solubility and therefore their toxicity. *In general*, fritted lead is considered safe if there are two molecules of silica, SiO_2, for every one molecule of lead oxide, PbO, *but this is only a guide and not a hard-and-fast rule*. Every supplier who sells frits, by the way, has molecular formulas for them and can tell you what the silica-lead ratios are. So frits are safer but not necessarily nontoxic. Where does this leave us? To my mind there are no reasons to have to use raw lead compounds, since leaded frits work just as well for fired results and are much safer to handle. This is particularly true in a classroom or a shared studio.

For the undaunted who will use raw lead in their glazes, the following precautions are advised for your health:

1. Wear a respirator made especially to filter lead or any toxic dust. Eliminate as much dust as possible by keeping lids on containers and *easing* raw materials into them, not dropping them.

2. Wear clothing that you put on only when you are using lead glazes and that remains in the studio after you are done mixing.

3. Wear surgical gloves if there are any cuts on your hands.

4. Wash your hands, especially under the nails, immediately after using and mixing lead glazes. A shower later on is a good idea.

5. Have no food, drink, or cigarettes around when lead or a lead glaze is used.

6. Do not spray lead glaze, even in a spray booth.

But if you use lead frits you'll be saving yourself a lot of trouble and anxiety, although it is not a bad idea to follow these same rules even when using most glaze materials.

Lead is not the only source of malaise for

the ceramicist. *Cadmium-selenium*—which colors the bright red and orange glazes—is also highly toxic, as is *potassium dichromate*, used for greens, reds, and oranges in some glazes. *Copper carbonate* and *barium carbonate* are poisonous materials, too. Use them cautiously, with reasonable care, and you will have no problems.

In making any glazes you should always wear a respirator, for the dust from any ingredients can cause lung disease. Silica causes the well-known *silicosis*, but there is an ——osis disease for almost every material you can breathe into your lungs.

Now that I've increased your life expectancy, let's worry about the people who may use your functional wares. If you are making things that could possibly be used to prepare, store, or serve food or drink, don't use raw lead glazes on the surfaces that would come in contact with the food or drink. Weak acids in foods such as tomatoes and oranges will dissolve the lead out of the glaze and carry it into the body. And unless you are willing to have the fritted lead glazes you make tested for lead release by a laboratory, I would avoid using them also. It's just not worth the risk when suitable replacements can be found. Commercial glazes, having been laboratory tested, will state on the label whether they are safe for food surfaces or not. These tests measure the *acid resistance* of lead to see how much will dissolve in a weak acid. If you are using a commercial fritted glaze that has tested safe for food, there are several factors to maintain the safety of the glaze.

1. The glaze must be fired to at least the cone number specified on the label, as the oxides need enough time and temperature to complete their safe fusion. The higher it is fired, the safer a glaze becomes.

2. Copper should never be used either over, under, or in a lead glaze if its lead release is to be kept to a minimum, since copper greatly increases the solubility of lead.

3. The thinner the glaze on the clay body, the safer it is, because the outside surface of a thick glaze doesn't interact with the clay body the way the inner surface does, and therefore remains more susceptible to being dissolved by acid.

4. Don't mix two lead glazes that have been tested safe. The result may not be.

Cadmium-selenium glazes are subject to the same dissolutions as lead and there is no way to make them safe. So never use these brilliant red and orange glazes on food or drink surfaces. Commercial glazes will be labeled if they contain cadmium-selenium.

The last safety measure I want to mention concerns the firing of lead glazes. When lead is heated, it tends to volatilize—that is, part of it changes to vapor and circulates through the kiln and *possibly outside it*. You want to ensure that these vapors have a quick exit out of the room the kiln is in. The best solution is to have a hood over the kiln vented out the ceiling, but this is often impossible or too costly. Opening some windows will provide enough ventilation to clear the room. Lead vapors may, however, hang around in the kiln and affect later firings. This is particularly true of electric kilns, which are much more static than gas-fueled ones. To clear electrics, leave the door open about 4 inches and turn all switches to high for about 2 hours.

Glaze Types

Alkaline Glazes

Alkaline glazes generally produce soft, scratchable surfaces that craze because of their high coefficient of expansion. They depend on *sodium, potassium,* or *lithium* for their flux. Because these fluxes are very active, alkaline glazes tend to be glassy and may run in the firing if slightly overfired. The good news is this: they result in intense, brilliant colors when mixed with coloring oxides. Even when used in glazes fluxed by other oxides, the alkaline fluxes can help brighten glaze color.

Frits are the best sources of alkaline metals for low-fire glazes. The feldspars contain too much alumina and silica for these low-fire glazes, and other sources are very soluble. Pemco Frit 25, Hommel Frit 259, and Ferro Frit 3185 are easily obtainable commercial frits that are highly alkaline and good starting points for alkaline glazes. All of them, in fact, will function as glazes at cone 06, but should be mixed with 2 percent bentonite for better adherence to clay bodies. If soluble salts such as pearl ash or soda ash are used to make glazes, they should not be applied to greenware, as they will be absorbed into the body and cause cracking during firing. It is best to use glazes with soluble salts on very hard bisque.

Boron Glazes

Boric oxide is a strong flux that is often used in glazes, particularly when trying to avoid the use of lead. All its sources, except colemanite or gerstley borate, are soluble, so it is a commonly fritted material. Boron produces a harder surface than either high-lead or high-alkaline glazes, and it can produce good brilliant colors. When used as a base glaze, it tends to get milky and sometimes blushes blue. It is often necessary to give high-boron glazes a longer firing time than lead glazes, because they tend to boil and need the extra time in the kiln to heal the glaze surface.

Lead Glazes

As noted, lead contributes to bright, glossy glazes with soft surfaces that tend not to craze. Without colorants, lead glazes tend to yellow. It's also important to remember that lead glazes, unlike alkaline and boron, will blister easily when in contact with flames, so they usually require electric-kiln firings, though this is less true of fritted lead glazes— which you should be using anyway to avoid raw lead.

One out-of-the-ordinary glaze virtually dependent on lead-based materials is *aventurine*. Aventurine is a crystalline glaze which develops small gold crystals when cooled slowly enough after reaching its hottest temperature. Lead seems to help develop these crystals. Anyone interested in pursuing this should read *Glazes for Special Effects* by Herbert H. Sanders.

Glazes on Parade

Several of the following glazes are adapted from Richard Behrens's glazes; others have found their way into my notebooks over the years.

Alkaline Glaze Recipes

cone 06	semi matte	
Colemanite		38
Lithium Carbonate		10
Nepheline Syenite		5
Kaolin		5
Silica		42

cone 014	clear glossy	
Ferro Frit 3269		44
Pemco Frit 54		26
Lithium Carbonate		10
Kaolin		6
Silica		14

cone 06	clear glossy	
Pemco Frit 25		95
Wollastonite		5
Bentonite		2

cone 06	clear glossy	
Boric Acid (dry)		7
Ferro Frit 3269		61
Kaolin		5
Silica		27

Leadless Barium

cone 06	matte	
Nepheline Syenite		12
Barium Carbonate		50
Boric Acid		20
Kaolin		10
Silica		8

Fritted Lead

cone 06	matte	
Hommel Frit 71		65
Kaolin		5
Barium Carbonate		8
Feldspar		22

cone 04	glossy	
Ferro Frit 3304		75
Ball Clay		25

Leadless Rose-Petal Red Glazes

cone 015	glossy	
Ferro Frit 3134		25
Hommel Frit 259		45
Lithium Carbonate		10
Kaolin		5
Silica		15

cone 06	glossy	
Pemco Frit 25		40
Pemco Frit 54		25
Lithium Carbonate		10
Kaolin		15
Silica		10

To produce the color add from 0.1 to 0.5 percent AuCl, gold chloride, to either of these glazes.

Fits and Faults

We've talked about how important it is to get a wet glaze to adhere to greenware or bisque-ware, so it should be no surprise that an "adherence" factor continues through the firing and cooling of the clay and glaze. This phenomenon is known as glaze *fit*. With two different materials, the clay body and glaze, expanding and contracting at different rates during the heating and cooling of the kiln, and the bubbling up of gases from both, it's no wonder that some weird things can happen.

Crazing

When a glaze develops a network of fine cracks, it has contracted more than the clay body during the cooling cycle. This means the glaze has a *tight fit*, is under a lot of compression, and relieves the pressure by cracking. As mentioned, alkaline glazes usually craze, lead glazes don't. The *crazing* pattern is, however, prized by many people and encouraged for decorative purposes; in such cases a glaze is more positively named a *crackle glaze*. The cracks can be stained and highlighted by rubbing ink into them or soaking a piece in strong tea or coffee. If you want to correct crazing, the addition of silica to either the clay or the glaze or the use of a finer meshed silica can help. With alkaline glazes, however, you may have to just learn to love it.

Shivering

Shivering is the opposite of crazing and occurs when the clay contracts more than the glaze during firing and cooling, resulting in a *loose fit*. You'll know you have shivering when pieces of the glaze begin to fall off the fired clay. Remedying it is fairly easy—decrease the silica in the glaze or in the clay body or increase the amount of alkaline flux in the glaze.

Crawling

Crawling is what happens when glaze beads up in some areas of the fired surface and exposes the clay body in other areas. Any dust that is on the clay surface at the time of glazing can cause crawling. Thus all pieces should be cleaned before glazing either by blowing with forced air or by lightly sponging with clean water. Another source of crawling in low-fire work comes from underglazes that are applied too heavily or not given a hardening-on firing.

Crawling is also associated with glaze materials that have high shrinkage rates, particularly plastic ball clays, zinc oxide, and colemanite. If a glaze develops cracks in the raw state on the piece, rub the cracks together with your fingers. Crawling is generally very rare in transparent glazes and much more common in matte glazes and glazes high in clay or colemanite. Try adding methocel binder to a crawling glaze to get it to adhere properly.

Pinholing and Cratering

Tiny holes or pits in a glaze are usually caused by gases bubbling up through the surface of the glaze. Generally, but not always, the glaze has time to smooth over these pinholes. Again, matte glazes suffer most, transparent glazes rarely. If pinholing does occur, you can:

1. Reduce the speed of the firing, fire a little hotter, or "soak" the ware for an extra half hour at its top temperature;

2. Substitute frits in your glaze recipe, since frits have already gone through a gas-releasing stage in their preparation;

3. Decrease the thickness of the glaze application; and/or

4. Avoid fluorspar and cryolite in your recipes.

Getting It On

Glazes are divided into three specific categories: *underglazes*, *glazes*, and *overglazes*. Their names indicate how they function relative to each other, but it is just as important to know how they function relative to the clay. Glaze can be applied to a piece when the clay is in any of three states: *green*, *bisque*, or *glazed*.

Green, you'll recall, is the state in which clay is air-dried but not yet fired. This is the most fragile condition the clay can be in, since it has none of the resiliency of its plastic state nor any of the hardness brought about by firing.

Glazed ware results when a glass-forming glaze is fired onto the clay.

Bisque (rhymes with *risk*) is what the clay is called after it has been given a preliminary or *bisque firing* to harden the clay body so it can be handled more readily, yet leaving it porous enough to accept underglazes and/or glazes. Once a clay body is fired to its maturing temperature (recall the absorption tests done in chapter 1), it is very difficult to get a glaze into its pores. So a bisque firing is usually done at a temperature lower than that required to mature the clay. For example, if a tested clay body has 0.5 percent absorption at cone 05, I would bisque fire it around cone 010. On the other hand, if a talc-ball-clay body has an absorption of 13 percent at cone 05, and I wanted to use a cone 05 glaze on this clay, I would bisque fire it to cone 1, where it still has 9 percent absorption and enough porosity to be able to accept the glaze easily.

With whatever clay body you use, you'll need to test fire not only its maturing temperature, but also a bisque temperature that allows easy application of glazes. The porosity of bisqueware is particularly critical in determining the thickness of application of some glazes: the more porous the clay, the easier it will accept a glaze, the thinner the glaze can be. Glazes are prepared with water, so thinning them is no problem. Bisqued pieces can be lightly sprayed or sponged with water before glazing, to ensure that too much glaze isn't absorbed. You will quickly learn by sight and touch how thick your glazes ought to be.

Many commercial potteries often break these general rules, by bisque firing unglazed ware to maturing temperatures that are higher than any of the subsequent glaze firings. They do this to help eliminate glaze faults such as pinholing and crazing and to be able to support shapes, such as plates, that are more susceptible to warping during hotter firing. When a glaze is fired it becomes molten so that it will stick to whatever it touches. That is why a support system can only be employed when there is no glaze on the ware (see photoessay on Richard Shaw, page 40). If at some point you run into any of these problems or find you have inadvertently fired your unglazed bisqueware to maturity, remember the following tips:

1. Glaze will adhere better to a warmed surface.

2. Glaze will adhere better when applied by spraying.

3. The thicker the glaze the better it will adhere. (The addition of methocel or bentonite will help thicken a glaze.) If the glaze has some clay in it (usually ball clay or kaolin), it can also be deflocculated in order to thicken it. Any deflocculant—including borax, calcium chloride, vinegar, Calgon, and soda ash—can be used for this purpose. Use from .02 percent to .05 percent of the total dry weight of the glaze batch.

A Special-Effects Glaze Technique

David Middlebrook uses the following technique to simulate polished stones, particularly turquoises, in some of his low-fire sculptures (see Plate 16), but it certainly can be used for many other applications requiring a variegated color surface.

The selection of glazes used for this technique is made on the basis of color, and though Middlebrook chooses to work with commercial glazes, your homemades will work just as well. Just make sure to use the same firing temperatures for all the glazes.

Pour the glazes out onto wax paper, each glaze forming its own patty about 1/8 to 1/4 inch thick. Since the glaze needs to be somewhat thick, you might let it air-dry in its jar with the cap off or use a hair dryer on it. Leave the patties to dry and then heat them in a kiln up to about 400° F. (You can do this in an electric kiln by firing on medium-low for about an hour.) Then slice the resultant hard patties into slivers with a scalpel or X-acto knife. So you now have thin slices of many colors, which you laminate onto an area of a bisqued piece, choosing the colors as you go. To make them adhere to the clay surface, wet the back side of each with a wash made from bentonite and water. Let the glaze slivers dry and then sand them with very fine sandpaper, smoothing the edges together. Then fire the piece slowly up to temperature.

For Middlebrook's particular objective of simulating turquoise, the laminated section is sandblasted to remove the glassiness from the surface and then polished with jeweler's rouge.

Underglazes

Underglazes are essentially coloring oxides and stains in special glaze bases. They are usually used to decorate greenware and bisqueware before any glaze is put on, making them, really, vehicles for color. Formulated to adhere to green or bisque pieces but without enough flux in them to become glossy, underglazes depend on a clear glossy *glaze* used over them to bring out their full intensity of color and seal them to the clay. Why not just put the stains and colorants into the clear glaze and forget about underglazes? Because as part of a glossy glaze, the colorants would *flow* with the melting glaze, moving wherever it moved. The idea behind underglazes is for them to stay where they're put, making hard-edge design and brushstroke painting possible. With just the right amount of flux and special preparation, underglazes will hold fast to the clay surface without being marred or blurred by the melt of the glaze put over them. Because of this, underglazes can be used like paint or watercolors. Intermixing doesn't always work as expected as far as the color is concerned, but there is no chance of the resultant underglaze running off the piece during firing. If you work this way, your glaze surface begins to achieve *depth*, one layer on top of another, and yet fused to each other.

It is not impossible to prepare underglazes at the studio level, but it requires so much grinding and firing that it is best left to the many companies who make and sell them commercially. A limited palette of underglaze colors can be made by using two parts colemanite to one part oxide or stain, but these will not have the smoothness of commercial products.

Colorants or stains are mixed with *flux* and some refractory material like kaolin or alumina that helps keep the underglaze inert. The mixture may undergo several washings, hundreds of hours of grinding, and be calcined several times. *Calcining* is the application of enough heat to a material to drive off chemically bound water; in this case the underglazes are fired in kilns until they begin to fuse, almost as if they were being fritted. The many grindings leave the underglazes smooth enough to flow easily and allow for fine brushwork and detail on clay surfaces.

When you begin to see the complexity involved in formulating underglaze colors (and we are just touching on it) you become thankful for the chemical wizards who make our technicolor visions possible. Each underglaze is put together to produce one particular color, and that color is dependent not only on the coloring oxide or stain but on the other ingredients in the underglaze mixture as well.

If colors are sensitive to chemicals within the underglaze, you'd be right in assuming they will be sensitive to chemicals the underglaze comes in contact with. So the wizards can't make them foolproof, and we need to follow some general guidelines for the use of underglazes.

One of the factors controlling the outcome of the fired color is the *atmosphere* in the kiln in which they're fired. Very simply, the normal firing of an electric kiln never starves any of the clay or glaze materials of *oxygen*— there is always enough for whatever chemical reactions take place. This is called an *oxidizing* atmosphere. In fuel kilns, such as natural gas or propane, it is possible to starve the interior of oxygen, either by cutting the flow of oxygen or by increasing the amount of fuel. In any case, the result is a *reducing* atmosphere, where the unburned carbon combines with oxygen in the glaze, affecting the results. Lusters, considered in the "Overglazes" section, depend on reduction firing. Commercially available lusters now have local reducing agents in them, so it is unnecessary to reduce the kiln in which they're fired. Many high-fire colors, particularly copper and iron reds, are also dependent on a reducing atmosphere. As noted, lead glazes are very sensitive to reduction firing, and are blistered and blackened by them. Gas kilns can be fired in oxidation, but often the burner flame will cause some discoloration when it comes in contact with underglaze or glaze. (For a fuller discussion of kilns and firings see chapter 5.)

In general, underglazes will work best in oxidizing atmospheres. If you are working with a store-bought glaze and don't know what's in it, you'll obviously have to run tests to see what results it produces when used to cover underglazes.

Underglaze Colors

Blue underglazes usually contain cobalt oxide or carbonate, both strong colorants. The blue stains are often made by fusing cobalt and alumina, cobalt and silica, or vanadium and zirconium. The lighter shades are produced by modifying cobalt with nickel, iron, and/or manganese. Covering glazes that contain zinc oxide tend to produce blue-greens, light blues, and violet-blues when used over blue underglazes. Phosphoric oxide and boric oxide in a glaze will push the blues toward violet, while sodium and potassium sometimes shade the blues toward ultramarine. Good blue colors can be achieved with either lead or leadless covering glazes. Blue underglazes are not much affected by the atmosphere in the kiln.

Green underglazes are usually made with chrome, although moss greens are produced by praseodymium phosphate and some bright greens make use of a zirconium-vanadium and tin-vanadium mixture. Covering glazes with zinc oxide or tin oxide may diminish the brightness of chrome green underglazes, while the presence of calcium, barium, and magnesium can intensify them. Most greens need oxidation firings.

Yellow underglazes derive their color from lead-antimony, tin-vanadium, praseodymium, or zirconium-vanadium stains. Except for zirconium-vanadium yellow, which fades under lead glazes, all yellow underglazes are very reliable and stable, mix easily with other underglazes, and work well under most covering glazes. They are not very sensitive to kiln atmospheres, so oxidation firing in gas kilns can give good results.

Burnt orange underglazes are made with a chrome-iron-zinc stain. *Bright orange* and *bright red* are produced with cadmium-selenium and are too sensitive to be used as an underglaze. (If you want these brilliant colors, you'll need to use a glaze or china paint.) The underglaze oranges, though, are very dependable in gas or electric kilns and mix well with other underglazes.

Red and *pink* underglazes are derived from several stains: chrome-tin, chrome-alumina, manganese-alumina, and zirconium-iron. Chrome-tin is the usual stain in most underglazes, resulting in brick reds, maroons, pinks, and violets. Flesh and salmon shades result from chrome-alumina stains. Most red underglazes are sensitive to kiln atmo-

sphere—pink being particularly sensitive—so that a very clean oxidation firing is necessary to get good results. Lead or leadless cover glazes will work, but chrome-tin colors are sometimes affected by the presence of barium oxide and/or magnesium oxide in the covering glaze, and zinc oxide will prohibit most pinks.

Brown underglazes are produced from chrome-iron-zinc and manganese-alumina stains, the latter for red-browns. Lead or leadless cover glazes work well with them, in either gas or electric kilns.

Black and gray underglazes are made from the oxides of iron, chrome, manganese, and cobalt, carefully blended so that no one color predominates. Black underglazes are so loaded with oxides that a little goes a long way when mixing black with other underglazes to darken them. Blacks and grays can be fired in gas or electric kilns.

White underglazes are usually made with the opacifier tin oxide. White mixes readily with other underglazes, and is used—much as white paint mixed with other paints—to give lighter shades. Whites have no firing problems.

Underglazes are made in several different ways, each of which provides a particular approach to the decoration of ceramic forms.

Underglaze Chalks and Pencils

Underglaze *chalks* come in the usual stick form, and can be used much like normal chalks or pastels, rubbing with a finger to create soft edges, or rubbing colors together. Most of the chalk underglazes are light or pastel colors, but don't fire out quite as subtly as they look, though the thinner the cover glaze the better the results. This is generally true of glaze applications over underglazes, and fritted glazes are best, since they can be applied very thinly and still provide a good glassy surface which brings out the underglaze colors.

Underglaze *pencils*, which look like standard colored pencils, come in shades of red-brown, brown, green, blue, yellow, and black. They can be sharpened and used for outlining, accenting, shading, or drawing like normal pencils (see Al Widenhofer's "Tornado Deco," Plate 2). The color range is severely limited, but can be supplemented with other forms of underglaze or overglaze.

Underglaze pencils and chalks will work best on smooth bisqued clay, since using them may require a little more pressure than you'd like to put on a piece of greenware. In order to ensure a very smooth drawing surface, the clay body should have very little sand or grog in it. After bisque firing your pieces, you can carefully sand them with very fine sandpaper. Then be sure to remove all traces of dust and grit so that the clay surface will remain smooth and glazes put on later will flow evenly.

Both underglaze pencils and chalks tend to be very dusty themselves, and designs made with them can easily be marred in handling. To prevent this, do a hardening-on firing—a firing to red heat (cone 010 or hotter) that adheres the underglazes to the clay body—after you've finished with your pencil or chalk design.

Liquid Underglazes

After undergoing hundreds of hours of grinding and being mixed with water or sometimes glycerine, underglazes are incredibly smooth, but still need to be stirred before you use them. Experience will tell you how thick they should be for the kind of application you want to do. There are two general types of liquid underglazes: translucent and opaque.

Translucent underglazes, like watercolors, have a thin, see-through quality to them. They can be used *over* one another very effectively, since their translucency allows whatever is beneath them to show through. (See Patti Warashina's pieces, Plates 3 and 4.) Translucents can also be mixed together or used over opaque underglazes.

Opaque underglazes are much more concentrated than the translucents and therefore give solid coverage. When working with opaques you'll have better color control if light colors are worked into the design first and then the darker colors used over them where needed.

B.T.U.: Buying, Testing, Using

After reading the description of how different underglaze colors are made you should realize that there are few choices a manufacturer has in order to produce certain colors. The bases that the coloring oxides and stains are mixed with (i.e., fluxes and/or alumina and/or silica) can vary somewhat, as can the *amounts* of oxides or stains used in each, but in general, all are produced similarly. I've always intermixed different colors and brands without any problems. So beginning users of underglazes shouldn't worry about which company's underglazes to buy. With experience your preferences will surely develop, but for now work with as many or as few as feel comfortable. Most ceramics-supply stores carry only one or two brands of underglaze, so you might want to check out a few stores.

Before using underglazes on green or bisqued pieces, you should test each underglaze on tiles made of the same clay body as the pieces you want to underglaze. Start by brushing a band about 1 inch wide of each underglaze color onto the tile. You can overlap each color to see if that brings any spectacular results. Mark each color on the tile so you know what you've done. (You may want to assign each a number or letter and keep the code in your notebook.) The marking can be done with underglaze pencil or by brushing on iron or cobalt oxide mixed with water.

After firing the underglazes onto the body, try different glazes over them—a leadless glaze, a fritted lead glaze, or a raw lead glaze—to see what differences in colors occur. Save these tests, as they'll tell you much of what you need to know before you start to glaze your pieces.

If you are going to use *brushes* to apply underglazes on your clean, dust-free green or bisqued pieces, you might want to work from a palette rather than straight out of the bottles, as you can then start to intermix and thin the colors as you would paints, without contaminating the sources. You also might find it handy to make the underglazes even smoother for brushing by adding glycerine to them. Also, a 25 percent solution of methocel in water added to the underglazes will harden them on the piece and make them less susceptible to smearing and smudging. Too much binder, however, can cause blisters during the firing, so use it with caution. Underglazes can also be applied with an airbrush (see page 118) for smooth shading and color gradation. Underglazes need to be thinned with water and should be strained to remove any lumps before being used in an airbrush.

Once you have finished your underglaze design, I strongly recommend doing a hardening-on firing to ensure that any glaze you put over it won't smear or wash away any of the colors. You may find, in fact, in the course of airbrushing a piece, that you'll need to do several hardening-on firings in order to mask sections off and keep any unwanted underglaze from getting on them. For simpler shapes, masking tape can be used to cover certain areas, but for more complex designs *liquid latex* can be used (see page 121). After airbrushing, the tape or latex needs to be pulled off the masked area. If the underglazes haven't been fused to the clay body, there's more than a good chance they'll come right off when you pull.

Too heavy an application of underglaze could cause peeling or chipping in the glaze fire, or even dirty the color and cause crawling of the cover glaze. Too heavy an application of cover glaze will start to move the underglazes.

Overglazes

Overglazes are normally applied to the surface of a fired glaze and fused to it by another firing. They are generally fired at much lower temperatures than other glazes, between cone 015 and cone 020, which provides for some dazzling colors and sheens unobtainable in any other way. Like underglazes, overglazes require so much time and special equipment to prepare that it is best to buy them already made. After the relative cheapness of clay and glaze materials, however, it's always somewhat shocking to find out what overglazes cost.

Because of the very low heat needed, most overglazes can be fired to maturity in a kiln in three to four hours without damaging the pieces they're on. Most cracking problems result from too rapid a cooling, but you'll need to determine a schedule for your particular clay body and the shapes you make from it. Flat shapes like plates and large tiles are more likely to crack because they sit on such a large area, preventing even distribution of heat. Plates can be put on stilts or clay supports for overglaze firing. Because of the low heat, there's no chance of the plate distorting. I've done two-hour overglaze firings on tall pieces made of both vitrified and open bodies, cooled in two hours, and had no problems. Some people, on the other hand, take several days to fire and cool china paints.

Keep It Clean

Using overglazes is one endeavor where neatness still counts. Overglazes by nature have big egos and want to be the center of attention: they're brighter than everything around them. This means, of course, that any imperfection is magnified and almost certainly will become the focal point for anyone looking at a piece. Lines that are meant to be straight and unblurred should be straight and unblurred, perhaps necessitating the extra effort of masking off their edges before applying the overglaze. At the same time, you need to make sure that the colors you apply don't *spot* during firing. Discolored spots are usually caused by dust, cigarette ash, breadcrumbs, or excess moisture settling on the overglaze before it's fired, or from the overglaze being applied over dust or greasy fingerprints. If the piece has been sitting around the shop awhile, it's a good idea to clean it with lacquer thinner or acetone before overglazing it.

Metallics

Gold, silver, copper, platinum, palladium, and bronze are the metals used to make *metallics*, which, after firing, leave a thin coating of the metal on any glaze surface to which they've been applied. The metals are mixed with flux, oils, and binders to facilitate application and fusion to the glazed surface. Metallics are opaque after firing, and they will have the same finish as the glaze they're put over, matte or glossy, and reveal any texture or crazing in the glaze.

Metallics can be used without trouble over all glazes, although some green glazes will discolor them upon firing. These should be tested beforehand. Platinum is normally used to create a silvery finish, as actual silver tarnishes easily.

Metallics *don't mix*, so if more than one is to be used on a piece, they should not overlap or touch. They can, however, withstand more and hotter firings than lusters (see next section), so if using both metallics and lusters, fire the metallic first, then do the luster in another firing. You can use the lusters, then, over the fired metallics.

The firing temperature for metallics is directly affected by the glaze on which they're put. A cone 05 glaze requires a cone 019 or 018 metallic firing. For a cone 1 glaze, the metallics can be fired up to cone 014. Because of the oils and binders in the metallics, the kiln needs to be well vented during the entire firing. If using an electric kiln, you should keep the lid propped open about five inches throughout the firing. The fumes and smoke need somewhere else to go, for they will damage the elements of the kiln and dull the finish of the metals. Gas kilns fired in clean oxidation can also be used to fire metallics.

The metallics come in small vials and are fairly viscous. All of them can be thinned with *gold essence*. If a metallic needs thickening, pour out what you need on a palette and let the thinner evaporate until it is thick enough. Metallics can be brushed, sponged, or airbrushed. Tools can be cleaned in lacquer thinner and should be rinsed several times, as any residue left on the brush or in the airbrush will mix and discolor whatever it's used for next. Don't use brushes that have been used with china paint, for any china-paint residue will discolor metallics.

If the results of your firings are *purplish*, you didn't get the metallic on heavy enough. Reapply and fire again. If the metallics turn out *dull* or *cloudy*, either they were on too heavily, or the kiln wasn't vented enough to allow the vapors to escape. If you didn't fire the kiln hot enough, the metallic will rub off easily. If you fired it too hot, the metallic will be crazed.

Lusters

Lusters are also thin coatings of metal which get fused to the surface of a glaze. However since lusters fuse in a way different from that of metallics, they can not only reproduce the appearance of the metallics, but can also provide many other colors and sheens.

The original luster technique, developed by the Persians, was to brush metallic oxides directly on the ware, and then smoke the kiln at the end of the firing cycle and during cooling to reduce the oxide to bare metal. A more recent offshoot of this ancient method is *flash luster*, whereby the metallic oxides are incorporated directly in the glaze, thus eliminating the need for a second firing. These flash lusters also require a reduction atmosphere during the cooling cycle of the kiln firing. Herbert Sanders, in his book *Glazes for Special Effects*, deals with both these processes in detail.

Another firing-oriented luster process is achieved by *fuming*. In this technique, the glaze firing is done to whatever cone the glaze matures at. The kiln is then allowed to cool to dull red heat (around 1000° F), and *tin chloride* is thrown or sprayed into the kiln, where it volatilizes. The fumes then fuse to the surface of the glaze, creating a silvery mother-of-pearl color. This is not as brilliant a luster as that achieved by direct application, nor can you predict or control where it will fume the pieces in the kiln. It's best used when it won't detract from a hard-edge design. Keep the kiln closed tightly during fuming, and stay away from any fumes given off. A tablespoon or two of tin chloride will suffice for a small kiln of up to 20 cubic feet. These fumes are very hard on the elements of electric kilns, so this technique is not recommended in them. *Strontium nitrate* and/or *barium chloride* can be added to the tin in order to get a little more color. (See the photoessay on Bill Abright and his raku firing, page 125.) You can also get the same casual blush or highlight on a piece by airbrushing commercial lusters and doing a second firing instead of this fuming process.

The modern commercial technique for making lusters takes advantage of local reducing agents, so that luster firings can be done in oxidizing kilns. Most lusters are made with a resin, usually *gum dammar*; a metallic salt for color; a flux, usually *bismuth nitrate*, zinc oxide, and lead oxide; and an essential oil, turpentine, or oil of lavender. The resin and oil act as the reducing agents, thereby depositing the metal on the surface where it's fused by the flux.

Lusters come in what seem like minuscule bottles for outrageous prices, but need be applied only very thinly, so a bottle will last quite a while (unless, of course, you're covering huge areas).

Lusters can be applied with soft small brushes or with airbrushes. As with the metallics, the brushstrokes should not be gone over repeatedly. Heavy application of some metallic lusters may lead to running, making them easier to rub off. Lusters contaminate particularly easily, so airbrushes and brushes should be rinsed with acetone several times after using. Many people abide by a "one

brush for every luster" rule, but with a little care it's not really necessary. If you want to thin the luster for airbrushing, do it with *luster essence* (oil of lavender) or acetone.

Lusters don't mix and shouldn't touch if two are applied to the same piece. The general firing range for lusters is from cone 020 to cone 018, regardless of the glaze they're used over. Since they are easily damaged by second or third firings, it is wise to save the luster firing until last. Lusters, like metallics, need good ventilation: fire electric kilns with the lid or door propped open about 5 inches. If you are worried about cracking, you can close the lid a little after the kiln is shut off to slow down the cooling.

Aside from the metallic lusters, the two basics are mother-of-pearl and opal. These two will give a rainbow sheen to a glaze without changing its basic color. The advantages of using these instead of fuming are the control they afford, the deepness of their sheen, and the ease with which they can be fired. They can produce some very subtle effects when used on some glazes and dazzling effects when used on others, particularly over fired metallics. The metallic lusters are sold in almost all supply stores, but some of the colored lusters, like red and orange, may be harder to find, since their shelf life is only two or three months. If you discover any, be sure to test it before using it on good ware.

If the luster rubs off after firing, the application was too heavy. A blue cast is caused either by fingerprints or brushes contaminated with other lusters or metallics. If little color is gotten, the luster was put on too thinly or the kiln was overfired.

China Paints

China paints are produced much like underglazes, except that they are formulated to melt and fuse between cone 019 and cone 016. This very low melting range is produced by using a higher percentage of flux—primarily lead and/or boron, sodium and potassium—than in underglazes. Coloring stains make up from 10 to 50 percent of any china paint. Kaolin or aluminum hydroxide is added to produce a matte or vellum surface. Because of the lower firing temperatures, brighter colors are produced, particularly from cadmium-selenium stains, which result in bright reds and oranges.

Like underglazes, china paints can, in general, be mixed together, either on the palette or directly on the piece, making the subtleties and tonalities of oil or watercolor painting possible. For the most part the colors in the raw state approximate the fired colors, but these will vary with the temperature they're fired to and the glaze they're used over. Violets made with gold usually appear gray-violet in the powder though they fire out to the deepest of violets. Generally, yellows fire out darker than they appear. The definite exception to the mixability of china paints (and you will discover others that don't work, either to your expectation or satisfaction) are those reds and oranges made with cadmium-selenium. They can be mixed among themselves with good results, but not with other colors. They are also very sensitive and unstable at temperatures higher than cone 016; I would recommend firing them at cone 019 or 018. They must be applied heavier than the other china paints in order to get any color. They also have a better chance if done in quicker-than-normal firings. Fire the kiln up to cone 019 in two and a half to three hours with the lid cracked 3 or 4 inches.

The traditional firing range of china paints is from cone 019 up to cone 016. Most colors will remain stable however, up to cone 013, where they interact a little more with the glaze they're put over. Some, though, will start to lose a little color by then. Blues and purples can stand the heat, reds and oranges can't. Test firings are always in order when trying hotter firings or mixing untried combinations. For the most reliable colors, stay in the lower range.

China paints are normally used over glazed surfaces and are translucent, i.e., they take on the quality of the glaze. They can, however, be very effective over fired clay, in which case a matte texture develops. If subsequent layers of china paint are fired on, the surface smooths to a satiny finish. You can also buy ready-made matte china paints if you prefer a non-glossy finish. Some of the paints have more flux in them than others, so they will give a glossier surface. This is particularly true of black and the dark blues. If you want to increase the gloss of any of the paints, however, a small amount of a specially prepared *china-paint flux* can be ground into the powder and oil during mixing.

Many of the techniques of china painting or airbrushing rely on several firings of the same piece because most of the china paints can stand it. The exceptions are the cadmium-selenium colors; blacks, which tend to start flaking off after three or four firings; and some of the blues and greens, which tend to get darker after several firings.

Mixing It Up

China paint is sold in two forms: premixed and powdered. The premixed comes ready-to-use in jars and tubes but does not generally offer the selection of colors that the powdered paints do. However, many shades can be made by intermixing the existing colors. These premixed colors are usually of a consistency perfect for silkscreen application, but need to be thinned with *turpentine* for brushing. *Acetone* should be used when quicker drying is desirable, as with airbrushing.

The powdered china paints are sold in small glass vials or can be bought in bulk, which is a good investment if you plan to do a lot of china painting. There are scores of colors of china paint made commercially in powder form, and mixing them is the beginning activity for most china painters—it establishes a rhythm the way the wedging of clay does before the clay is actually used.

The mixing is done on a *palette*—which can be a piece of glass, a glazed tile, or even a flat plastic lid—with a *palette knife*, a standard painting tool.

Oil is the normal *medium* for binding the china paint, enabling it to adhere to a glazed surface. There are many oils that will work, even special china-painting mixtures you can buy. Three of the more popular oils are *French fat*, *oil of lavender*, and *copaiba balsam*. You can use them separately or together. Each will give a different thickness to the final mixture. French fat is the thickest and stickiest of the three oils.

The china-paint powder is tapped out of its vial onto the palette. Experience will teach you how much powder to use for a particular area you want to paint, and you'll get such experience from preliminary testing. Add enough oil to grind the powder into *paste*. Generally, the oil required for this is about half the volume of paint. Some pigments, usually the dark blues and violets, need a little more oil than others. Don't, however, use too much oil, as it could cause the china paint to boil during firing. With the palette knife, grind the oil and powder on the palette in circular motions, making sure each grain of paint is crushed. This should take only a couple of minutes, but the longer you work it, the smoother it becomes. Some colors are grainier than others, particularly the pinks and purples and some of the blues and greens, and may need to be mixed a little longer.

Gum turpentine is then added to the ground china paint and oil to thin it to a working consistency for brushing. Turpentine dries rapidly by evaporation, so you can keep adding to the paint as you need it.

Mixing for Airbrush

China paint should be mixed a little heavier until it's a thick paste on the palette, when it's to be used with an airbrush (see page 118). A few drops of ceramic silkscreen medium can be added to the powder-and-oil mixture to help it adhere and dry quickly on a glaze surface. This can then be scraped off the palette into a small jar or cup and thinned with *acetone*. (Acetone dries more quickly then turpentine, and gives the paint less chance to run.) The final solution should not be very thin—about the consistency of half-and-half.

If any china paints remain on the palette after you've finished using them, they can be covered with thin plastic and set aside. To reuse them, just add enough solvent to get the right consistency.

China Painting

With china paints it is possible to go back into the design, firing after firing, to delay finishing the piece until you're absolutely satisfied with it. Aside from improving the color range, working with overglazes puts one in closer touch with the actual finished surface than does working with underglazes, especially if clear glaze is used to finish the underglaze surface. Once that's on, it's impossible to get back into the underglaze design or painting. If the clear glaze has changed some of the colors after firing, there isn't much you can do about it, unless you want to start covering up with overglazes—and then you're working on a different surface.

China painting requires the same basic skills and color sense as any painting medium, although the details of techniques, of working on a glassy surface, really need to be developed through experience. Regardless of whether you want to do the flora and fauna of traditional china painting or are aiming closer to the ozone, the knowledge that you need—which has been compounded over the hundreds of years of the art's existence—may well rest in your local hobby-shop instructor. On the other hand, the information provided here, together with your own experimenting, testing, and gradually getting a feel for the medium, will allow you to work comfortably and proficiently with china paints.

China paint can be applied by brush, airbrush, or with a piece of silk wrapped around cotton. Because it is used on an already fired glaze or clay surface, it tends to go on thinly and resist absorption. In general this is fine, as china paints don't need to be thick to be effective, except for cadmium reds and oranges. As indicated previously, thickening the mixing oil enables you to get heavier applications. Too heavy an application, however, will cause running during firing or even during application. Normally, layers of paint are built up through multiple firings, working from light to dark. It's very easy to darken a light color, but a lot of work to lighten a dark color—though the results can be worth it, which explains why some traditional china painters do work from dark to light colors.

Use good clean brushes to apply china paints on a fired surface. Brushes can be cleaned with turpentine or acetone, and afterward should be conditioned with a little mixing oil. Brushes made specifically for china painting are available, though any good brush, especially sable, will certainly do. Brushes come in many sizes and qualities, and are usually numbered; the smaller the number, the shorter and thinner the brush hair. Painting on a glazed surface is like ice-skating, since the brush is not impeded by the texture of paper or canvas, and thus may take some getting used to. Good brushes help.

The surface to be painted should be made absolutely clean by rubbing it with acetone or denatured alcohol. The alcohol, by the way, if left on without wiping and allowed to dry, makes the surface easier to sketch on with a regular graphite pencil. This can be of some help in laying out your design. The pencil marks will burn off during firing, as will those of special china marking pencils.

China painting is especially effective for developing rich surfaces because of its ability to be layered with or without intermediate firings. *Shading* or *shadowing* large areas with small brushstrokes or with an airbrush gives added depth, regardless of design.

If you want to shadow at the edge of the color, either brush or airbrush another coat of the same or a darker color. This can be done either while the first color is still wet or after it's dried, but do not apply it so heavily that it

will run in the firing. (You can also play it safe by firing the first color before working in the shaded area.) If you are working wet, all colors you want to use should be ground and mixed on a palette before you begin.

An airbrush will give very subtle color gradations if you *overlap* the spray at the edges of other colors. (For more on airbrushing, see page 118.) These same gradations can be approximated with brushstrokes and *blending*—use a small stiff brush to apply overlapping colors as Xs, then carefully blend the X strokes by dabbing with a piece of silk wrapped over a ball of cotton.

Dabbing china paint on a large surface with a piece of silk wrapped around cotton is called *laying ground*. This is a useful way to cover a large area with color, though traditionally it was used to apply a background for a darker-colored motif. When laying ground, the china-paint powder should be ground with a little extra oil and *no* turpentine. Five or six minutes of grinding is recommended for smooth application.

China-Paint Colors

There are many manufacturers of china-paint pigments. Since the colors, like glaze and underglaze colors, are made by many companies, there are many different names for the same colors, although there are standard names for some shades, like blood red, apple green, albert yellow, and violet of iron. Most colors are made in light, medium, and dark shades.

Iron Reds are the blood reds and red-brown shades. They will lose their color during firing if put over wet unfired yellows. If the yellow is fired on first, though, these reds will hold their color. When they are mixed with gold reds, the gold reds will predominate.

Gold Reds give many shades of pink, rose, violet, ruby, and purple. These colors are expensive because gold is used as the colorant.

Cadmium-Selenium Reds are the brilliant reds and cannot be mixed with non-cadmium-selenium colors. These reds need to be applied a little heavier than the other china paints and should be fired only to cone 019 or 018.

Cadmium-Selenium Oranges are the brilliant orange colors that cannot be mixed with non-cadmium-selenium colors. These, like the reds, need a little heavier application and should be fired to cone 019 or 018.

Oranges other than the brilliant cadmium-selenium are known as yellow-red or light carnation.

Yellows can often cause problems for other colors used around them. Pale yellow is usually referred to as ivory yellow or primrose. Darker yellows are known as egg yellow or albert yellow. Yellow china paints are particularly sensitive to heavy applications and will blister during firing.

Yellow-Greens are called moss green or the darker Meissen green.

Greens are very dependable china paint colors. The lighter shades include apple green and bright green; darker shades are called dark green or velvet green.

Other colors that are fairly dependable include: blue-greens, blues, purples, browns, grays, flesh, whites, and blacks.

Ceramic Decals

The decal is a means of transferring a prefabricated design or photograph to an area where the design is wanted. You've probably already used many decals in the nonceramic world, mostly on car windows, proclaiming your vehicle to be legally registered or proclaiming yourself to be a "Mad Dog of Blessed Springs University." The same and, thankfully, other applications can be made on fired clay.

Ceramic decals are made by the same processes as other decals except that china paints are used instead of inks. Once the decal is applied to the clay piece, it is treated as china-paint decoration and fired between cone 016 and 019 to fuse the design to the clay or glaze surface. It is possible to make decals with underglazes, but all commercial ones are made for overglaze application and firing.

Decals open up a new realm of surface decoration. They are made by silkscreening, though some of the more complex commercial decals are done by lithography. Drawing on curved vertical glazed clay is hardly an ideal way of working on a hard-edge drawing. It is much simpler to execute a drawing on paper and then make it into a decal that will readily conform to the curving shape of the piece. Old and new photographs can also be reproduced in this way. And, the silkscreen/decal image can be repeated as many times as you want. In this sense, decals are to glazing what plaster molds are to forming—they offer possibilities achievable in no other way, and yet can easily be abused to give endless repetition of one design.

Buying and Ordering

If you decide to work with ceramic decals, you can either depend on standard commercial decals, send camera-ready copy to decal companies and have them make your individualized decals, or make them yourself.

Several commercial firms produce decals you can buy at hobby shops and ceramic-supply houses. Often, however, the selection of these distributors is very limited since they don't carry most of the thousands of decals printed. Usually each store will have a catalog you can order from, but you can also write to any of the companies to buy a catalog. There is usually a minimum order required, so if you don't want to buy a hundred dollars' worth of decals right off the bat, maybe you can start a decal cooperative with some friends. That way you'll get direct service and cheaper prices.

Most commercial decals are of the flora and fauna of traditional china painting or corny cartoon characters hitting golf balls, brilliantly colored fish and butterflies, or dark Renaissance paintings.

Making Your Own

Making ceramic decals involves two other mediums besides china paints: photography and silkscreening. You can avoid the first but need to learn the second. It is possible, and done often in industry, to silkscreen glaze, underglaze, or overglaze directly onto a ceramic surface. But for the studio person, this application is generally limited to flat shapes.

Here is a brief summary of the making of a one-color decal:

1. The image to be transferred is made into a *positive transparency*, either a halftone or continuous-tone. (You can do this yourself in a darkroom or have it done for you by a printer or anyone else performing camera work.) The most common positive transparency is called a *PMT* or photochemical transfer.

2. The positive transparency is then contact-printed onto a photosensitive film (stencil) or exposed directly on the screen with a photosensitive emulsion.

3. If using a stencil, it is adhered to the silkscreen.

4. The imageless border of the screen is blocked out.

5. China paint or underglaze is prepared and squeegeed through the screen onto decal paper.

6. After the color is dry, a layer of clear oil-base or lacquer-base medium is applied over it.

Preparing Artwork: The Film Positive

You can draw, paint, print, or photograph a silkscreen decal. Photographs are already camera-ready copy and can be made into halftone film positives (see below). All other artwork should be done on white paper with black ink for high contrast. Light blue ink or pencil will *not* show up under the camera, so it can be used to establish margins and outline the components of the design as well as for writing instructions to the printer.

If the design or image contains only black and white—that is, positive and negative—areas of whatever color, or if you want your final decal to be high-contrast without grays or in-between tones, you can make (or have made for you) a *continuous-tone film positive*. However, if you want subtlety of gradation, particularly in photographs, a *halftone positive* is required. Halftone is the process that breaks an image into small dots. There are many different dot patterns to which an image can be reduced. Each is measured by how many dots there are per inch. The more dots, or lines, as they inappropriately get called, the finer the reproduction of the image. Halftones of 65, 85, 100, or 120 lines per inch are good for decal purposes.

If you have access to a darkroom and equipment and want to do the film positive yourself, either continuous-tone or halftone, you can learn more about the process from two Eastman Kodak booklets, *Basic Photography for the Graphic Arts* and *Halftone Methods for the Graphic Arts*. Otherwise take the artwork to a print shop, which can make the film positive for you.

The Silkscreen

Here again you have the choice of saving time *or* money: you can easily make your own silkscreen—consisting of a rectangular wood frame with silk, nylon, polyester, or metal screen stretched over it—or buy prestretched screens from screen-process suppliers.

You can make the screen frame from fir or pine 2-by-2-inch or 2-by-4-inch lumber. Miter and join the corners, the way picture frames are made. The frame, and therefore the screen itself, should be a couple of inches larger all the way around than the image to be reproduced. You can print more than one image on a screen at one time as long as you want them all the same color. The frame should be very tight with no wiggles at the joints. These should be white-glued and then nailed or screwed since the screen must be tightly stretched over the frame, exerting a lot of tension on it. An easy way to get good screen tension is to use *Easy Stretch Cord*, available at graphics-supply stores. The cord and screen edges are pushed down into a groove cut in the frame.

There are several screen materials and many mesh sizes to choose from. The choice is made according to the kind of image you're printing. The three general types of materials are: silk; metal, mostly stainless; and synthetic, mostly polyester and nylon. The stainless and synthetic screens are monofilaments, though there are some polyester screens available in multifilaments, the way all silk comes. Monofilaments have thinner thread structure, thus allowing more color to pass through the screen, producing finer images. Screen-printing stencils, however, adhere better to silk. But silk is also more easily worn from the abrasive action of the china paint than is polyester, nylon, or stainless. Here then, are the recommendations for screen materials and sizes:

For Printing Continuous Tones:	Silk 14XX Nylon, Polyester, or Stainless 170 to 200 mesh.
For Printing Fine Design Halftones:	Silk 16XX Nylon, Polyester, or Stainless 200 to 250 mesh.
For Printing Clear Coat:	Silk 8XX or 10XX Nylon, Polyester, or Stainless 86 to 110 mesh.

The rule-of-thumb for printing halftones is that the mesh of the screen should be *twice as fine* as the halftone, e.g., for a halftone of 100 lines per inch, a screen of 200 mesh is used.

After your screens are made (and remember you need a separate screen for the final clear coat over any decal you print), an area needs to be set up where the printing will take place. Here again, cleanliness counts: any dust that settles on the china-paint decals will burn the color out. Printing should be done on a smooth, level surface—you might construct a *baseboard* at least a couple of inches larger than any screen you use. The baseboard can be made from smooth ¾- or 1-inch particle board or plywood covered by a smooth surface like Masonite. *Clamp hinges* are used to secure the silkscreen to the baseboard while allowing it to lift from the front for the placing and removal of decal paper. You will also need a *squeegee* the right size for your screen.

Preparing the Screen

It is especially important to roughen the fibers of a new polyester or nylon, but not silk, screen in order to help the film stencil adhere to it. This is done by rubbing *powdered carborundum* onto the screen. Every screen, however, should be degreased just before the stencil is applied. This is done by rubbing *trisodium phosphate* on the screen with a brush and then rinsing it off.

The Stencil

One way to transfer the photopositive film (contact-printed onto the stencil) to the silkscreen is to use a stencil, in this case a photosensitive film backed by some heavier support like Mylar or plastic. Here is a good method:

1. Lay a sheet of black felt down on a clean work surface.

2. Put the stencil film, shiny or plastic side *up*, on top of the felt.

3. Place the positive transparency, with the correct image side *down*, onto the shiny or plastic side of the stencil. This means the reversed image will be facing *up*.

4. Lay a sheet of plate glass over the positive transparency. This should be enough weight to keep the positive flat against the stencil.

5. Position a sunlamp bulb directly over the top of the glass, about 2 feet from it. Six to seven minutes' exposure from the sunlamp (ultraviolet rays are needed, so a heat lamp won't work) will give an excellent stencil. You should do test exposures, however, with any stencil film you use, as exposure times vary from stencil to stencil.

6. After exposure, place the stencil in *developer* recommended by the makers of the stencil film, who will also tell you how long to leave the film in the developer.

7. Then wash the stencil film with running water. The emulsion will have hardened on those areas struck by the ultraviolet rays, that is, the clear areas on the film positive, and remained soft (and will wash out) on the darkened areas. In other words, there is now a *negative* on the stencil.

8. The film will be sticky when wet. Place it right side up on a clean work surface or baseboard. Lower the degreased screen onto it, making sure it is centered or at least positioned where you want it. Gently blot the screen with clean newsprint (not newspaper), changing sheets until the screen is dry.

9. The margins on the screen around the stencil now need to be sealed so the china-paint ink can't get through during printing. This can be done with a water-soluble liquid blockout poured on and smoothed with a small piece of cardboard or rubber spatula. The first coat is put on the back of the screen and allowed to dry.

10. Carefully peel the plastic backing off the back of the screen. Then smooth two more coats of blockout on the inside of the screen, letting the first coat dry before applying the second. If you get any of the blockout on the areas of the screen that should print, take a wet paintbrush and brush it off. Seal the edges of the screen, where mesh meets wood, either with masking tape or a sealer like *Pro-Seal*.

Erasing Stencils and Films From Screens

When you have had enough of one design and want to free the screen for something else, you need to clean all the film and emulsion off it. The blockout will come out with running water. With polyester, nylon, or metal screens, household bleach or acetone can be used to remove stencils. *Don't use bleach on silk* or you will destroy it. You can clean silk with acetone or hot water and a scrub brush, or take it down to the do-it-yourself car wash and run the high-pressure hot water through it.

Mixing China Paints: Another Way

Making decals requires that a substantial amount of china paint be pulled across a silkscreen and that it be thicker than for brushing or airbrushing. This doesn't mean that a lot more gets used per square inch of area decorated, but rather that a lot of it must be available for spreading over the screen. In any case, you can't afford not to buy your china paints in bulk or use premixed paints such as Amaco's *Versacolors*.

You can continue to mix on your palette of glass or tile, or, since you'll be making up larger quantities, you may want to use a porcelain *mortar and pestle*. Make up as much paint as you want and store it in airtight jars.

A clear ceramic decal lacquer is usually needed to mix china paints for silkscreening since the typical oil used with china paints is too runny and doesn't dry fast enough. Acetone, on the other hand, dries too fast and would clog up the screen—and dissolve the stencil. You can experiment with different vehicles, but try to use the same medium for mixing china paints that you use for the final cover coat. This will ensure that you have no problems from different shrinkage or boiling rates during firing. Some mixing agents will not absorb enough pigment. This is especially critical with cadmium-selenium reds and oranges. The pigment-to-vehicle ratio will have to be determined by experimenting, though a good place to start is by trying two parts pigment to one part vehicle. See if it goes through the screen and what kind of fired color you get from it.

If you use a lacquer-base vehicle, you can add some *butyl lactate* to the mixture to help keep it from clogging the screen. Use about 28 parts by weight butyl lactate to every 100 parts of dry weight of china paint in the mixture. The consistency of the "ink" should be fairly thick. Experience will teach you the exact thickness that works best for you.

If your ink smears, it is probably too thin and should have more china paint in it. If it gets too thick and doesn't move correctly or go through the screen, more vehicle is needed. At the same time, remember to test fire the mixture to see if your colors are right.

If you desire to color your decals with underglazes, you cannot use the ones prepared with water unless you dry them out thoroughly—possibly in the low heat of the kiln for a couple of hours—and then regrind them with vehicle. You can also buy powdered underglazes in bulk from a supplier.

Paper and Printing

Decal paper is normally a single sheet of heavy porous paper which has been coated with a special gum that releases the decal when submerged in water. The paper is known generically as *simplex*.

Because the decal ink is very sticky, a *vacuum table* is a great help when printing since it keeps the decal in place. It is, however, another expense, and instead you can use a spray adhesive on the baseboard to help stick the decal paper to it.

Even if you are doing only one-color printing, it is good practice to keep each sheet of decal paper in the same place when screening so that each one can be gone over again with a clear coat of your vehicle after the china paint dries. Keep the paper in place with *registration marks*. After you've centered and adhered your first sheet of decal paper, mark off the bottom two corners with masking tape, making right angles at the vertical and the horizontal edges. Then line up all subsequent

sheets of decal paper for that particular run in the same position as that first one. You can also buy commercially made *registration tabs* which glue down to the baseboard and into which the corners of decal paper will slip. Registration becomes critical when doing more than one color, since you need to realign each decal sheet to print the other colors without overlapping.

To print, place the decal paper in the registration marks, shiny side up, and pull the screen down flat. Put the mixed china paint at the top of the screen, all the way across, and with a squeegee, pull down with one medium stroke, moving slowly but steadily. As you print, the ink may start to thicken. Adding fresh ink will help thin it, but you can always return the ink to a jar and add more vehicle.

After printing, lift the screen, take the decal paper off the board and let it dry. Do your entire run. When the ink is dry, change to a coarser silkscreen and pull a coat of clear-coat vehicle over each decal. The area of clear coat should be larger than the image but smaller than the decal paper. This will protect the china paint and become the means of transferring the image from the paper to the clay piece. After this coat has dried, store the finished decals between sheets of plastic or waxed paper.

A Two- (or More) Color Decal Process

Making decals that have more than one color requires a separate stencil and screen for each color used. For complex halftone printing, in order to have the different film positives with which to make up the stencils, this means having to send your artwork out to a company that does color separations. Color separations can get rather costly. However, if you are doing continuous tones or want to use continuous areas of color on halftones, you can do all the color separations yourself.

Following is a description of a two-color process that worked very successfully for ceramicist Richard Shaw (who is featured in one of the photoessays in this book).

Shaw found a Blue Goose Pears label that he wanted to add to his decal "vocabulary." There are two colors, orange and blue, in this design, so he needed two pieces of film that separated the areas that were to be printed in the two colors. He achieved this by having both a *positive film* and a *negative film* made of the label. If he had wanted even more colors he could have made more positives and negatives and blacked out certain areas with the use of self-adhesive colored acetate sheets such as Rubylith or Zipatone. (Smaller areas can be blacked out with black acetate ink.) It is important to keep all the separations you make aligned so that colors will not overlap when they're not supposed to. When doing the separations, you always need to remember that any area that appears dark in the film positive or negative will allow color through the screen, and any area that is light won't.

Wilson Burrows is a silkscreen artist whose studio is in Bolinas, California. Working with Shaw on this project, he prepared two screens, one using a stencil made from a film positive and the other made from a film negative. Both screens are 200-mesh polyester monofilament, chosen because of the crisp image obtained and because silk tends to sag after some use.

The screens are prepared by rubbing powdered carborundum on them, rinsing them with water, scrubbing them with trisodium phosphate, and again rinsing them clean with water. The screens are then set aside while the stencils are made.

Burrows has made a contact-printing table for himself from a piece of framed glass hinged to a work surface which can be clamped tightly shut while he prints under ultraviolet light. To bring the film stencil into tighter contact with the film positive or negative when the glass is lowered onto them, he uses felt and cardboard on the table surface. He has placed a sunlamp directly over the table, which is connected to a wall timer that automatically shuts the light off after seven minutes of exposure.

Before contact-printing, Burrows mixed up the stencil film developer for use with the Ulano Super-prep film stencil. He prefers this film because of its wide exposure latitude. While other films may have sharper printing characteristics, they are also much more sensitive than Ulano Super-prep to any dirt that happens to be on the film positive or negative. The developer, an A and B powder, is mixed then put into the developer tray and covered. It should be kept out of strong light.

The film positive and negative are contact-printed onto stencil film and soaked in developer for ninety seconds, one at a time. Each is then taken to a source of water—in this case, Burrows's bathtub—and rinsed. The water should be fairly warm to begin with, approximately 90°F, and then cooled as the gelatin of the stencil is rinsed away, so that by the time the stencil is cleaned the water is at about room temperature. The stencil is then washed for thirty to sixty seconds after everything appears to have been rinsed off.

The wet stencil is then placed on a clean sheet of Plexiglas, and the prepared silkscreen is laid over it. Laying the stencil down on Plexiglas, or even on a piece of cardboard to raise it off the table, helps give better contact because the screen can bend around it. Newsprint, rubbed gently with a cloth, is then used to blot the stencil and screen dry.

After this preliminary drying, a coat of water-soluble blockout, Superblox, is applied to the back of the screen. This keeps any ink from coming through the margins of the screen where there is no stencil. After this first coat of blockout dries, the plastic backing sheet is removed from the front of the screen, which allows the first coat to dry before the second is applied. The perimeter of the screen is sealed with masking tape. (Remember that Burrows is preparing two screens for printing with two colors.) While the screens are drying, the decal paper is cut and the registration on the printing table set up.

Each sheet of simplex decal paper is measured and cut to a size just a little larger than the image to be printed, leaving an inch or two border. Burrows then makes up a "dummy sheet" to set his registration marks—critical in printing more than one color. The dummy sheet is made up of the positive and negative films, taped in place on a sheet of drawing paper cut the same size as the decal paper. He positions the dummy sheet on the printing table and pencils in his registration marks on the table. Each sheet of cut decal paper is then laid in the same position and marked. In this way the penciled registration marks on the decal paper will be in line with the marks on the table each time the paper is printed.

The first screen is then positioned on the table and aligned with the registered dummy sheet. The screen is secured to the table by clamp hinges attached to a length of narrow board that stretches across the table. The board itself can then be clamped to the table to maintain the screen's position. One set of hinges allows the screen to move up and down for printing and removal of decals, while the hinges on the board allow for easy interchange of screens. Wood blocks are then clamped to the table to help keep the screen in position.

The first screen is then ready for printing. The decal paper is registered on the table, the vacuum is turned on to hold the paper in place, and the screen is inked and then lowered. One slow and steady pass is made with the squeegee. Burrows applies a little diluted glue to a part of the screen that is allowing ink through where it shouldn't be. He did not do any floodcoating for these decals, though he often does. (*Floodcoating* is running the ink over the screen with the squeegee once, before lowering it and making a pass for printing on the paper. It will give you more ink, but can also smear the prints.)

As the decals are printed they are hung up by clothespins to dry and await the second printing. When they are dry, Burrows puts the other screen on and prints the second color, keeping a close watch on the registration of the decals. These are also hung up to dry, and when they are ready, another screen

is put on the table, this one a 10XX silk he uses for the final clear coat to cover the china paint.

Applying Decals

Whether your decals are homemade or store-bought, they should be stored in a safe, dry, and dustless place under waxed paper or plastic until you are ready to use them, since the lacquer or oil-base vehicle and cover coat will crack after long exposure to moisture, thus causing the china paints to crack.

Like any overglaze application, decals must be used on clean surfaces.

1. Place the decal in a bowl of warm water. It will probably curl up tightly immediately, but after about thirty seconds will start to unroll.

2. The area on the piece where the decal is to go should be cleaned and dampened with water.

3. Take the entire decal, backing and all, out of the water. Test to make sure the image is loose by pulling lightly at it. It should begin to slide off the backing. If not, put it back in the water. Don't force it, because it's easily torn.

4. Slide the decal off the backing onto the piece. It should slide considerably on a glazed surface so you can position it quite easily. If you are working on a very curved surface, you can warm the piece (around 90°F) to help flex the clear coat of the decal.

5. If you want to apply a decal to an unglazed surface, coat the surface first with white glue. But remember that large solid-color areas tend to crawl when applied on unglazed surfaces, though line drawings or printing work well.

6. Make yourself a paper squeegee, about matchbook thickness, and, starting from the center of the decal, squeegee out the

water from under it. Don't rub too hard or the decal will tear. If it does, don't panic; just realign the edges, making sure not to overlap them. Then use a cloth or paper towel to blot the decal dry. Get all air, water, and wrinkles out. They will burn the color out wherever they remain.

7. Let the decal sit for a day, making absolutely sure that all moisture evaporates from it and that no dust settles on it.

8. Fire the kiln as for any china paint, with lid or door open about 4 inches, to cone 019 to 016 depending on the colors of your decal. Remember that the cooling rate will also have an effect on the colors and sometimes on the clay body, so test the differences between cooling with the lid open and closed.

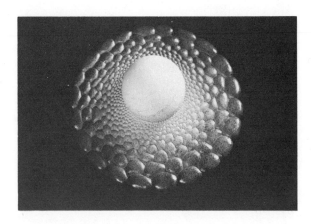

The tin outbuilding that Duane Ewing uses as a studio is about a thirty-yard walk from the house he lives in, tucked away in a secluded little valley in Sebastopol, California. His electric kiln has a very small room of its own attached to the studio.

"A.R.T. Dome"
by Duane Ewing

Ewing's recent work is dominated by handbuilt pyramids and slipcast low-rising humps. He often plays against the pyramid's symbolic longevity and spirituality to satirize our culture's dedication to consumerism and its chauvinistic belief in itself. One piece was made by joining crumpled slipcast Volkswagens into a perfectly smooth pyramid. Other works, though, use the pyramid just for its perfection and beauty of form, enhancing it usually by a repeated design carved into the surface of the clay.

The hump forms are made from a one-piece drain mold. The mold is a block of plaster that Ewing carved with a plaster tool into a concave shallow bowl or plate shape. The resultant clay cast from the mold is

turned over, making a smooth convex hump shape he likes to call an *antiplate*.

The piece seen in process in the photos is titled "A.R.T. Dome" and is based on an antiplate. Since he knew he wanted to carve the cast hump, Ewing made it thicker than he normally would to give himself enough clay to be able to carve deeply into the shape. To do this, he allowed the poured slip to sit in the mold longer than usual, checking it until the wall built up to the desired ½ inch thickness, before pouring the excess slip out of the mold.

Before the hump form was cast, however, Ewing had to make a new mold to obtain the dome shape he wanted. A trip to the local drugstore turned up a rubber ball just the right size. A cast taken from a mold of the ball would have the right proportions and would look good sitting atop the low-profiled hump.

A sturdy cardboard box served as a casting unit to make the mold of the ball, which was first set on a slab of plastic clay about the size of the box. The slab was about 2 inches thick at the start. More plastic clay was then added to the slab until the lower half of the ball was surrounded. The ball and clay were then dropped into the cardboard box, the clay corners smoothed and sealed tightly to the sides of the box.

Ewing then weighed out some plaster, added it to a weighed amount of water, and stirred by hand. For the final minute of mixing he placed the bucket of plaster on an old foot massager; this brought to the surface a few air bubbles, which he promptly scooped off. The plaster was then poured, filling the box to the top. A stick was used to smooth the top.

After the plaster set, the four top flaps of the box were taped tightly together. The box was then turned over, so that the bottom became the top. He reopened it and removed the clay, leaving the top half of the ball exposed and the bottom half buried in plaster.

Two keys in opposite corners were then dug out with a plaster tool and the hardened plaster surface was sized. He mixed more plaster and

poured it into the box, smoothed the top, and allowed it to set. After Ewing pulled the two pieces of the mold from the box, he carved a hole from the top surface into the spherical chamber, thus providing an opening to pour slip in and a drain to pour the excess out.

The casts of both the ball and the antiplate were made with a commercially prepared slip clay that Ewing later fired to cone 06. Although it's a very weak body, it allows him to sand easily after the bisque firing, a stronger consideration than strength for his nonfunctional pieces.

After removing both cast pieces from their molds, he spent about an hour getting the sphere into the dome shape he was looking for, cutting off about a third of the bottom before attaching it to the antiplate. Then he started carving.

Carving was a laborious process that required many hours of concentration (and, for Ewing, a lot of coffee). He was constantly picking and brushing the leather-hard clay, deepening the grooves that separate the stonelike elements, until finally a landscape that looked both organic and extraterrestial surrounded the dome.

The piece dried over a couple of days and was bisque-fired to

cone 06. Afterward, both the carved elements and the dome were carefully sanded smooth. Running water from an outside tap helped rinse any dust from crevices.

Ewing then proceeded to pick out thirteen underglazes from the many dozens in his studio. He ended up with several different commercial brands and a palette of oranges, reds, and yellows. Then started the long and painstaking process of dotting the dome. The underglazes were applied thickly, straight from the jars, a dot at a time from the very tip of a brush. This is similar to creating halftones, except that Ewing

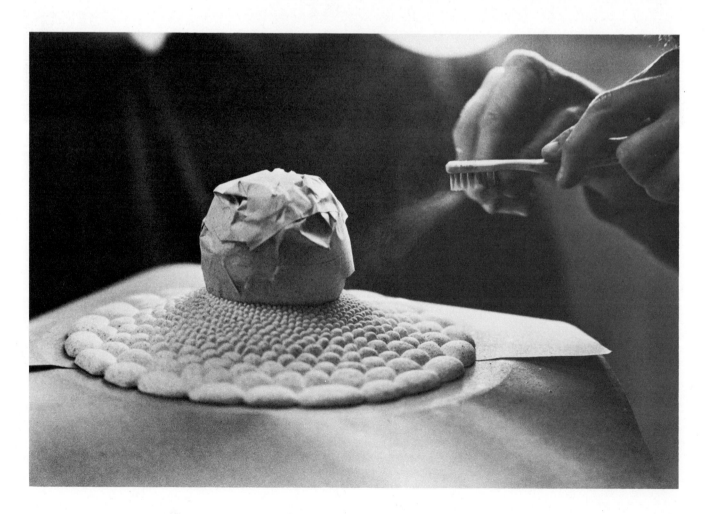

keeps the dots separated enough so each maintains its own color; at the same time they are applied thickly enough to rise above the clay surface instead of sinking into it. When the dotting was complete, the piece was fired again to cone 06 to fuse the underglazes to the clay. There are no glazes on this piece, just the dull finish of underglazes and the dull sheen of china paints applied to an unglazed surface.

First the dome was masked off with newspaper and masking tape in preparation for china painting. Four china paints were mixed on a glass palette. A mixture of French fat oil and balsam of copaiba was used as a medium, and then thinned with acetone. Ewing spattered the china paints onto the carved surfaces with a hard-bristle toothbrush. Sometimes he used a needle tool, and sometimes his thumb, but in either case the colors were flying over, onto, and about the piece, getting layered one over another into speckled patterns. He concentrated the paints on the larger outside stones and decreased them as he approached the dome and the tinier stones, looking to make a smooth transition from the china-paint spatter to the underglaze dots.

After the paper and tape were removed, the china paint was fired at cone 019. The results can be seen in color Plate 17.

5

Now We Are 06

In getting to the end of this book—after examining processes and techniques as well as some personal approaches to working—there are a couple of subjects I would like to expand upon, now that the basic concepts of low-fire ceramics are established. As you have probably realized, there is a step-by-step order in which work gets done. One method is chosen over another and used at a particular time on a particular piece. Learning that order and making those choices is as difficult a learning process as mastering the techniques themselves. Now you are ready to juggle four balls instead of three.

I attended a workshop at which a master potter who has been working in clay for a long time gave a demonstration of how he assembled a large piece from several pieces thrown individually on the potter's wheel. When he had joined the first three pieces the form was over two feet tall. He turned the chair he had been sitting in and propped one leg up on it to brace himself while he worked on the form spinning on the wheel. He turned to his audience and said: "Now you probably didn't take much notice of that, but it took me a couple of years to learn to move that chair like that."

You don't get information like that from books, but by *watching* what *you* are doing. Know as many techniques and processes as you can but don't lose sight of the *complete* process of being able to bring a personal order to all your technical knowledge. See the trees *and* the forest. Plant new trees.

The Airbrush

The application of stains, oxides, underglazes, and overglazes with an *airbrush* can bring about very subtle color gradations, give depth to surfaces through shading, and create graceful and flowing curves. Glazes themselves are usually too coarse and need a much thicker application than that afforded with an airbrush; however, some commercially made fritted glazes are milled fine enough and can go on thinly enough so they can be sprayed through an airbrush. With most glazes, a *glaze* or *spray gun* works best for covering large areas. They work on the same principles as airbrushes but hold larger quantities and have much larger tip openings for the thicker, coarser materials.

The airbrush itself is not a difficult tool to use, although it requires preparation, cleaning, and patience. But the payoff in surface enrichment and color control more than compensates for the time spent. The essentials are the airbrush itself and a source of air for it. Mandatory for your health are a respirator and spray booth.

The airbrush works on the same aerodynamic principles as an atomizer. Air passing over an open-ended tube stuck in a liquid will pull the liquid up the tube and force it in the direction the air is traveling. So an airbrush needs only two controls: one to let the air into the brush, and one to control the *amount of color* passing through its tip. (I will refer to the underglaze, stain, glaze, or overglaze used in an airbrush as *color*.)

The air pressure is set at the air source, either tank or compressor, so the control at the airbrush is really an all-or-nothing situation, though there is a little adjusting screw under the top button of most airbrushes that can, when raised, decrease the volume of air passing through the brush.

The control of the color, however, is all up to you. There are two types of airbrushes, which differ only in the ways they control color.

The *single-action* airbrush has a control button on top that is pushed down with a finger to allow the air through. The amount of color is controlled by an adjustable collar just below the tip of the brush. Tightened all the way, no color will flow.

The *double-action* airbrush has a single control button on top for both functions: press it down to allow air through, and pull it back to control the flow of color—the farther back it's pulled, the more color is released. The double-action kind costs about twice as much as a single-action one of comparable quality and will put your coordination to a real test. Once you master it, though, you will have better control. The single-action works just fine, however, and is recommended for the first-time buyer.

Interchangeable tips are made for single-action airbrushes, generally classified as *fine*, *medium*, or *broad*. The fine tip will not give wide coverage or much overspray and is used primarily for doing fine lines and dots. It tends to clog frequently with most applications, though it seems to work all right with lusters. The medium tip can give almost as fine a line and yet be adjusted for overspray and wider coverage. This is the tip to start with for most airbrushing. The broad tip won't give as fine a line as the medium tip but will cover a wider area. It's best used for spraying large areas. A nut on the back of the color adjustor/tip on some models, and a setscrew on others, unscrew so the tip can be removed for cleaning or changing.

Spraying

The shape of the color area applied to a piece—that is, a line, a dot, or a 4-inch circle—is determined not only by how much color you let come through the tip but also by how far you hold the airbrush from the piece while spraying. The spray expands from the tip in a cone shape, so the farther from the piece you hold the brush, the wider the area the spray will cover. The smaller the area you want to spray, the closer you hold the brush and the less color you allow through. With a medium or broad tip, hold the brush:

1. ¼ to ½ inch from the object for fine lines or dots; close color adjustor almost all the way.

2. ½ to 4 inches from object with stencils or for small areas or bands of color; allow more color to flow.

3. 4 to 12 inches from the object for general coverage, depending on size of area and how much overspray is desired; color should be adjusted toward open, all the way for the broadest coverage.

For some closeups—say within 2 inches—I'd suggest regulating the air pressure down since it can create waves in applied color by blowing the center covering out to the sides. You normally run an airbrush between 30 and 40 pounds of pressure. For closeups, decrease to 20 to 25 pounds.

While we're on the subject of air pressure, let me tell you how to get it:

1. You can rent a tank of compressed air if you know you'll have limited use for your airbrush.

2. You can buy a tank that has a fitting to receive air from a gas-station airhose or from friends who own air compressors.

3. You can buy a diaphragm compressor—the least expensive kind—which runs continuously, creating constant air pressure. Many ceramic-supply stores that sell airbrushes stock small diaphragm compressors.

4. You can buy or rent a piston-tank compressor, which will run until it builds up enough pressure in its tank, and then shut off. These are more expensive than diaphragm compressors and usually much stronger than necessary to run an airbrush. However, if you want to run several airbrushes at once, as in a classroom, this would be the way to go.

Regardless of the source of your air, you must have a regulator and air-pressure gauge so you will know how much pressure is getting to your airbrush and be able to adjust it. Some compressors have these built in, but you should check. The 30 to 40 pounds of pressure needed for airbrushing is relatively low, so a big compressor isn't necessary. If you adjust the pressure down to around 10 pounds, the airbrush will splatter the color much the way Duane Ewing does with a toothbrush (see page 114).

Before you start using the airbrush for your good pieces, a little pregame warmup is advisable. You can spray onto old newspapers or on pieces of broken bisqueware. With a single-action brush, start with the color adjustor closed and the tip about ¼ inch away from your target. Open the tip slightly and spray. Keep moving the airbrush back while opening the color adjustor to develop a good sense of how to regulate your distance and color and learn any idiosyncracies you or your airbrush might have.

Once you have the feel of the brush, practice your strokes. The smoothest way to apply color is to stroke it on the piece steadily in one direction and then back again. You can work from side to side, up and down, or diagonally, but try to maintain the same direction to get a smooth application. Press the air-control button down at the start of the stroke and release it at the end, to prevent color from accumulating and running at the edges of the sprayed area. It's cheaper, by the way, to use screened iron oxide and water than to waste your under- or overglazes during practice sessions. Since each material you spray will have a different viscosity, however, you should always take a few warmup strokes with the color you are going to use on your good pieces.

Every airbrush comes with at least one cup or jar for holding color. You can buy others that range in size from ¼ ounce to 4 ounces. The larger ones are very useful for covering large areas or spraying a lot of one color on several pieces.

To determine how thick your color should be, remember that it needs to be thin enough not to clog the airbrush, and thick enough not to run on the piece when sprayed. This usually means mixing it to the consistency of milk or half-and-half. Underglazes are normally thinned with water, china paints with acetone and a few drops of silkscreen medium, lusters with luster essence (oil of lavender). I recommend, though it's not imperative, screening the colors through about a 100-mesh screen right before using them. This will break up any lumps and ensure a smooth flow through the tip, preventing any sputtering. If you're using a larger jar on the airbrush, and some of the color material settles to the bottom while you're spraying, remove the jar and remix the color.

Cleaning

If you are using stains, oxides, glazes, or underglazes that are mixed with water, cleaning is very easy: keep a bucket of water handy. Remove the jar, leaving the cap and siphon in the airbrush. Any of the small open cups can also be left in. Place the cup or siphon tube into the water, open the color adjustor all the way, and run water through the brush until it sprays clear. You can spray this water onto some newspapers or a large sponge, or you can turn the brush toward the water and spray into it. The airbrush should be cleaned immediately after using it, or the color will start to dry and cake in the tip.

If you are using something other than water, like acetone or luster essence, to mix your colors, you cannot clean with water but need to use either acetone, turpentine, or mineral spirits. Again, the quicker you clean the brush after using it, the easier it will be. You can take the color jar off and replace it with a clean jar full of cleaning solvent. Run this through the airbrush onto newspapers. For overglazes it is particularly important to get

the tip clean, since subsequent overglazes used in the airbrush can so easily be contaminated. So take the tip off by undoing the little nut or setscrew at the back, and run solvent through or just quickly soak it in solvent. You can also use pipe cleaners to scrub the inside.

Safety

If you airbrush in your studio, you will soon be inhaling a fine mist of chemicals, and breathing will become a little more difficult. Even if none of the ingredients are toxic, the mist can, like dust, cut off your air supply. The fumes from overglaze vehicles can cause headaches and nausea. This can be alleviated by wearing a respirator and airbrushing in a *spraybooth*. A spraybooth is a partially enclosed area usually vented to the outside, and containing a fan to draw the spray from the front to the back or top, and out the vent. It's a good idea to have a filter or two—furnace filters work fine—to keep most of the spray from ever getting outside. After all, there are other people out there who have enough to worry about without getting another dose of lead or cadmium.

Portable spraybooths can be bought, or a very simple one built around an exhaust fan. Airbrushing is most comfortably done when the base of the object being sprayed is at normal table or workbench height, 30 to 36 inches off the ground. So a table 30 inches high and at least 3 feet wide and 3 feet deep can be built under the fan. On top of this table you construct the actual booth: two sides and a top, leaving the front open and the top of the table to serve as the bottom of the booth. The walls of the booth should then tightly enclose the exhaust fan. You can build a wooden frame and use just about any material for the walls, as they don't get much wear, though the surfaces should be cleanable. The front opening should be at least 4 feet tall, to allow you to do taller pieces and be able to move the airbrush around and spray from high angles. At the back of the booth, in front of the exhaust fan, build a frame to hold one or two filters tightly against all four walls, so no spray can get by without going through the filter(s). Remember to change these filters when they get clogged.

A useful airbrushing tool is the *banding wheel*, a raised lazy-Susan device, which makes it easy to turn the piece being sprayed without having to touch it and possibly mar the brushwork. The banding wheel can also help in getting an even application on large areas: spin the wheel with your hand and spray at the edge leaning into the spin (if it's spinning counterclockwise, this would be the right-hand side of the piece).

Edges, Stencils, and Masking

Soft edges are the wondrous creation of airbrush overspray, colors fading and blending one into another. This is not difficult to achieve but very easy to destroy by overworking the edges, applying too much color, and ruining their subtlety. Depth of color is better achieved by overlaying colors, mixing on the piece rather than in the jar. Sometimes it may be difficult to restrain yourself from working with untested color combinations on good pieces, but a good grasp of ceramics includes knowing enough to test *everything* first, and note all the variables. How was this underglaze applied? On what clay body? What went over it? How thick was it? To what cone was it fired? How fast was the kiln heated and cooled? Where was it in the kiln? Paying attention applies to all the processes, not just airbrushing.

Stencils can be a great help in getting particular shapes on the clay surface. Stencils work very well with airbrushing, though they can certainly be used with other color applications. They can be made from cardboard, thin acetate, thin brass, and thin, stiff plastic. The nonabsorbent materials should be blotted with paper towels after each use.

The stencil material needs to be malleable enough to conform tightly to a clay surface, so that when the color is applied, none will slip under the edges and smear. Usually, one hand holds the stencil to the clay, while the other hand is used to airbrush the color on.

Another aid in airbrush design is *masking*, or covering an area to prevent color from getting on it. The two materials usually used are *tape* and *liquid latex*. It is very important when masking or using stencils that the color from the airbrush not be thin and runny, or else it will creep under the tape or stencil. Liquid latex becomes fairly impermeable, however, so color thinness is not as critical when using it.

There are several kinds of tapes used to mask, the most obvious being *masking tape*, although *frisket tape*, available at graphics-supply stores, is nicer to work with. It comes in many different widths. Tape is usually used for masking straight lines, either negative or positive. If, for example, you lay a strip of tape down on a fired white glaze, spray apple green china paint all around it, then removing the tape and firing the piece, you'll have a white line on a green field. If, however, after you lay that strip down, you lay wide strips of tape along both its edges and then pull that first strip off and spray in between the two wide pieces of tape, the results after tape removal and firing will be a green line on a white field.

It is possible, though a lot of work, to tape an entire piece or a large portion of it, and then cut out those areas to be sprayed with an X-acto knife. It is much easier to sketch out the areas you want to color and then use liquid latex around them (see Photoessay on Bill Abright, page 125). Curved areas are *much* easier to negotiate with liquid latex than with tape.

Use only cheap synthetic brushes to apply latex, since it will destroy brushes. Have a jar of soapy warm water waiting when you finish brushing, and clean the brush immediately.

All masking material should be pulled off the piece before firing, as it will burn and blacken almost all colors and glazes in the kiln. All moisture on the surface of latex should be allowed to dry before pulling the latex off, as it could possibly mar the edges. And remember, any colors that you want to mask over must be fired on first, or the color will pull right off with the masking material.

Using the Kiln: Down You Go

By now you should be aware of the importance of kiln firings and the variables inherent in them. The history of ceramics, in fact, can be traced through the kinds of kilns and fuels used to achieve various results. For low-fire processes, we are concerned mostly with oxidation-atmosphere firings, and the electric kiln seems the best way to achieve them.

Beside its clean, dependable oxidation atmosphere, the electric kiln offers many advantages: it is easy to install, simple to operate, and takes up very little space in the studio or classroom. One convenient option on most medium-sized electrics is a *kilnsitter*. This is a device for shutting the kiln off automatically when it reaches the firing temperature of the cone. As the cone sags from the heat, a metal lever set on top of it also lowers and trips a switch that turns the kiln off. A kilnsitter is usually dependable and can be of tremendous use, but don't become so dependent on it that you leave a kiln to shut off by itself without checking. Stick around and worry about the pieces inside the kiln you spent so many hours making.

The cones used in kilnsitters are only about an inch tall, as opposed to the bigger cones you watch through the spyholes, which measure about 1¾ inches. With the kilnsitter you use only one small cone. If the firing is done visually—that is, by looking into the kiln through a spyhole to observe a cone bending—three different cones should be used. (This applies to any kiln, not just electrics.) The first is a warning cone to let you know the kiln is approaching the heat you want, the second is the cone you're aiming for, and the

third is a back-up cone to let you know if you've overfired. So if you wanted to fire a kiln to cone 05, you would place a cone 06, then a cone 05 and a cone 04 standing next to each other at about a 9° angle in a well-grogged wad of clay. Whether you use the large or small cones depends on how big the spyholes in your kiln are.

Now, most kilns fire unevenly. Most electrics will have a cone difference between top and bottom, so when cone 05 is melted on top, only cone 06 has gone down on the bottom. This varies, but until you know your kiln and glazes well enough, it's necessary to use two or more (depending on how large your kiln is) sets of cones. You can then decide whether to let the top go to cone 04 while the bottom gets to cone 05 or to turn the kiln off when the top is at 05 and the bottom at 06. Most low-fire clays and glazes have a good firing range—that is, they work over a two- or three-cone range. Once you know this is true for your clays and glazes, you can switch to working with only one set of cones.

Natural-gas or propane kilns can be used for clean oxidation firings or for those firings that need reducing atmospheres. Many older commercial potteries had gas kilns with refractory tubes (called *muffles*) running from top to bottom. These tubes, which contained all the flames and gases, radiated heat into the kiln chamber, and thus maintained an oxidation atmosphere. These kilns, however, were awkward to load and the muffles wasted much space in the firing chamber. In an open fuel kiln, *saggers*, or containers made of refractory clay, are still used to hold the ware, to protect the pieces from flame and smoke. (There are several books out that deal specifically with kiln building that can be of great help if you decide to build one for yourself.)

The placement of ware in the kiln is very important. To fire more than just one or two pieces at a time, *kiln furniture—shelves* and *posts* of varying sizes made of a clay body resistant to cracking—is used. Expensive silicon carbide furniture is really unnecessary for low-temperature firings. Most commercial kiln builders include shelves and posts with each kiln, or can sell them to you. Ceramics-supply houses also carry kiln furniture.

When stacked for bisque firing, pieces can be touching each other, and even sitting in one another if they can physically take the pressure. For a glaze firing, however, it's important to leave a little room around each piece and between shelves, not just to prevent pieces from fusing to each other, but to allow good circulation. Because of the reactive and volatile nature of some glaze materials, it is best to fire kilnloads of the same kinds of glazes. For example, try to fire all leaded glazes together and all unleaded ones in a separate firing. Fire cadmium reds and oranges separately when possible.

Your own firing schedule (including cooling) will have to be worked out according to test results: what happens to your clay body and what do your glazes look like?

Brick kilns and strict temperature measurements have not always been the only means of firing ceramics. Raku firing, such as Bill Abright's (see page 125), uses no cones, but instead depends on watching the glaze melt and become shiny. This and the immediate removal of the piece(s) from the kiln put one in a little closer contact with the firing process. An even more "primitive" way, still used in many cultures as the major means of firing, is the bonfire or *pit fire*. Pieces are laid on the ground or put into a pit dug in the ground, covered with pottery shards, and fueled by grass, twigs, or dung.

David Powers and I visited Dan Oberti the night he did a dung firing. The piece he fired was made on a potter's wheel using stoneware clay. This had been covered with white slip while it was still wet and then *burnished* when it dried. Burnishing is done with the back of a spoon or a smooth rock and gives the clay surface a shine.

The green piece was preheated in a small gas kiln to about 800° F. Oberti built a wood fire in a shallow pit and let it burn to hot coals. Wearing heavy asbestos gloves, he took the pot out of the gas kiln and placed it in the coals. From the small hill of dried cow dung he had collected from a local farmer, he selected and placed a small amount around and over the hot piece. This burned intensely for about half an hour. The piece glowed red-orange. At this point, Oberti grabbed the piece with his asbestos gloves and pulled it from the fire. The pot had large black shapes on the white background, recording where the pieces of cow dung had been placed against it and reduced it. Dan rubbed a dried piece of dung between his hands, crumbling it to dung dust, and danced around the piece throwing the dust on the pot as the spirit moved him. This smoked some of the white areas to gray and toned down the stark difference between the black and white sections. One of Dan's dung-fired pieces is shown in Plate 30.

Home Repairs

Making ceramic pieces is often an unnerving experience, given the vulnerable nature of clay in a dry or fired state. Each of us has his own bull-in-a-china-shop tendencies, and we often get a lot of help from friends, customers, leaping cats, and wagging dog tails. Then, of course, there are the natural drying and firing cracks we try so hard to avoid.

Sometimes the mends and repairs on a particular piece offer as interesting a personal record as the flame marks that leave their record on dung-fired ware—when R. threw her shoe at C. and hit the plate and cracked it in two. But everyone develops his or her level of acceptability: what's worth saving to some people gets tossed with the disposables by others. Passing judgments like this applies not only to wounded ware but also to those pieces you don't want to take credit for.

Remedies that follow are for that fragile world of ours, to patch, glue, and stick back together the best we can:

1. Vinegar and dry clay body make a thick slip for cracks in wet or leather-hard

pieces (which have become rigid but not dry).

2. Sugar, dry clay body, and water make a thick slip for cracks in leather-hard or green pieces.

3. Zircopax and calcined EPK with water and a few drops of sodium silicate make a thick slip for cracks in greenware.

4. One part Zircopax and one part silica with water make a thick slip for cracks in bisqueware.

5. Powdered bisqued clay body and grog with vinegar and a few drops of sodium silicate make a thick slip for cracks in bisqueware.

6. Ceramic-supply stores also carry patching materials; these as well as kiln cements will work on green or bisqueware. All usually contain sodium silicate.

Whenever dry clay body is called for, it is understood that it is the same clay body as the piece to be patched. The best procedure is to rub the elixir well into the crack and then sand it smooth. If the piece is still wet, slow down the drying by covering it in plastic. Anytime sodium silicate is used in a light-colored patching material, it will turn it dark gray. It will also fire and even dry so hard that it becomes difficult to get a glaze on top of it. These are things you should consider when doing this last-minute plea-bargaining.

Faking It

For those fired pieces that have cracked, chipped, or broken, and are not used for food or beverages, you can mend with:

1. Epoxy, either the 24-hour or 5-minute kind; dry oxides and stains can be added to the epoxy when you mix it, in order to match the glue color with a clay or glaze color. All clear epoxy tends to yellow after a while.

2. *Super Glue* can be used for nonporous clay bodies. It is much thinner than epoxy and so will conceal a crack much better.

In addition, you can touch up spots with acrylic paints or any of the many products for cars and boats. If you want to do large areas of a piece and glaze won't give you the surface you want, something like *Rub and Buff* might. It comes in many colors and is available at decorator shops. It needs to be put on some kind of primer, like *Prepareacoat*, which will keep it stuck to the clay body.

"Harvey's Bird"
by Bill Abright

Bill Abright shares an enormous warehouse space with a group of other ceramicists in San Rafael, California. The group situation allows each member to have his or her own work space and to share larger areas for glazing and kiln firing, activities which happen less frequently. A schedule is made up at the beginning of each month to assign each person kiln time. Since Abright is not doing any production, he rarely uses the large downdraft gas kilns but instead works in the kiln he built to fire individual pieces in *raku*.

Raku is a firing process derived from Japanese potters who originally used it to make ceremonial tea bowls. Today the process is widely used by studio craftsmen because it allows the maker almost immediate results and puts him or her into close contact with the firing process. Traditional firing and cooling can often take days, while a piece done in raku is placed in a preheated kiln and fired until the glaze is seen to melt. This takes from ten to twenty minutes, depending on the glazes, which are usually in the cone 010 to 06 range (although no cones are used during the firing). The fireman judges when the piece is ready by looking into the kiln and seeing how the glaze has melted and then pulls the red-hot piece from the kiln with tongs or thick asbestos gloves.

The raku process allows you to *reduce* the piece after it is pulled from the kiln and is still glowing. When placed in a container with some combustible material like newspaper or wood shavings, a clay body will be carbonized black, and any copper in or on a glaze will turn a red color or reduce all the way to the metal to give a copper luster. Sometimes the piece is doused quickly and fully in water to cool it and prevent the reduced colorants from reoxidizing. However, the piece can also be put in a smoking container and cooled slowly (a less severe shock than the water treatment) to prevent reoxidation.

You can understand, then, why a clay body used for raku must be open and porous enough to withstand the shock of the procedure. Usually a well-grogged high-fire stoneware clay is used to create pieces that are very fragile and brittle.

Most all of the forms Abright works with are started on the potter's wheel. He usually works by throwing several pieces at the same time (a throwing practice that is fairly common among people who use the

wheel to obtain some basic forms quickly). On the first day we photographed, he threw three large shapes, each out of 25 pounds of clay. One of these he pushed too far and it collapsed while he was throwing it. Of the remaining two he chose one to work on.

As Abright is very much concerned with space and flying—he does a lot of hang gliding—many of his pieces have birds or cloud forms on them. Yet he integrates that space by grounding the piece in the earth and fire of the raku process.

Lately he has been doing large raku bowls and building ritualistic grids with extruded clay "sticks" inside them. The grids seem like pyres that have burned and yet remain (which is in fact what happens to all fired ceramics)—a simple after-the-fact relic of the process as well as a record of it.

The first section of this piece was thrown into a modified cone shape, larger at the bottom and tapering in toward the top. This is the strongest physical shape and is needed to support the next section of clay.

The top of the first section was measured with calipers and a second section having the same top diameter as the caliper measurement was thrown. When the first section was stiff enough to support the second section, the bat that the second section was thrown on was inverted over the first section and the two pieces joined. The bat was removed from the top by cutting the clay with a wire. The two sections were thoroughly joined into one by making a pull up and a pull down between the piece while they were spinning on the wheel. This not only forced the two sections into one, but also thinned the piece.

To increase the drying time, Abright uses a heater on the outside of the piece. There are many people who throw large sectioned pieces and heat the piece from the inside, either by building a fire out of newspaper

or by dangling a lit electric light bulb down the inside. But this kind of drying doesn't suit Abright's purpose since it dries the bottom of the piece so much that it prevents the clay from stretching and giving in the later asymmetrical shaping he likes to do.

After the initial thrown shape is achieved, the piece is allowed to dry a little, just enough to still be malleable but not collapsible. Then Abright works on it with an array of wooden paddles and ribs, refining the form, giving it bumps and curves not possible with the wheel. With ribs he works on the form he's after by pushing the wall of the pot out from the inside. While doing the final shaping, he uses a mirror and black background—the mirror to help him see both sides of the piece at once, the black background to help him see the outline of the piece better.

A couple of coils of clay added to the top of the piece made it taller, and then Abright paddled the entire top somewhat flat. After some drying made the clay a little more rigid, he worked more on the top. He cut sections of clay out from each side, the negative shape following the bumps and curves of the piece, then added the birds. The bodies were tapered coils, the wings done in press molds. An excess of plastic clay was pushed into the mold and then cut flush with the plaster surface with a cheese cutter. The wings were picked out with a needle, left to dry a little, and then attached to the bodies that had already been connected to the piece.

Abright then dried the piece almost leather-hard and scraped it with a flexible metal rib to remove all throwing marks. He brushed on several coats of a white slip made from porcelain. This gave him a white surface to decorate with underglazes and ensured that the glaze he used over it would crackle, since he was looking for as much surface enrichment as he could find. The piece was then dried and bisque fired to cone 06.

As far as Abright is concerned, low-fire raku is a one-fire process that needs to be right the first time. His concern with surface quality and variation leads him to get the most out of his firings. Using slip, underglaze, airbrush, stencils, liquid latex, glaze, fuming, and reduction firing to carbonize and blacken areas left unglazed, he creates rich and varied surfaces. Any refiring in an electric kiln would reoxidize the blackened areas.

 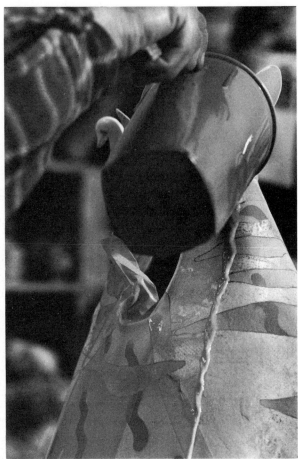

Abright spent about an hour and a half sketching in graphite pencil directly on the piece, indicating the shapes and areas to be left unglazed and those to be worked on. He outlined and changed large sweeping curves until they related better to the shape of the piece, the negative cut-out areas, and the birds on top.

When he was finally satisfied with the design, he brushed liquid latex on the areas that were to remain unglazed and therefore would be reduced to black in the firing process.

He then cut a piece of thin acetate sheet with an X-acto knife and made a stencil of a curvy, wormlike shape. Using an opaque purple underglaze, he airbrushed the worm shapes onto the piece to give the appearance of motion, as if the wavy lines were moving from the bottom of the piece toward the top. He held the airbrush with one hand, about 6 inches from the piece, and used his other hand to hold the acetate stencil tight against the clay surface. He used purple first since it was the darkest and strongest color and could withstand the subsequent overglazing from other lighter underglaze colors.

A light coat of opaque yellow underglaze was then airbrushed over the unlatexed portions of the piece, with the airbrush held about a foot from the piece while spraying. On top of the yellow, Bill airbrushed opaque ruby red underglaze, followed by light coats of purple, more red, and lastly yellow. This layering of underglazes created subtle color gradations and the illusion of surface depth. Bill then poured a thin clear glaze, made of 50 parts nepheline syenite and 50 parts gerstley borate, over the piece, controlling the pour for long drips on certain parts and no glaze over some underglazed areas. After the glaze dried, he pulled the latex off the piece.

By now night had fallen—fortunately, since the drama of raku firing is heightened by the darkened sky. Abright preheated his home-made gas-fired raku kiln. The bottom of the two-burner kiln is stationary, while the entire body can be raised by heavy cables that are strung over a pulley and attached to a counterweight.

Abright placed the piece on the bottom kiln shelf and lowered the kiln body over it (he had already measured to make sure the piece was

shorter than the kiln). He turned the gas up so the burners were roaring. Meanwhile, he prepared torn newspaper for the reduction and made up a squeeze bottle full of stannous (tin) cloride solution for fuming at the end of the firing. Twenty minutes later, Abright peered into the kiln and saw that the glaze was melted. He quickly turned off the gas, pulled down on the counterweight to lift the kiln up, and revealed the glowing orange-red piece. He sprayed the bottle of stannous cloride at the piece a couple of times and it rapidly volatilized, filling the kiln shed with acrid vapor. The poisonous stuff soon dissipated through the roof opening.

Bill donned his thick bandaged asbestos gloves, grabbed the piece, and carried it over to the waiting newspapers arranged in a large galvanized pan. The newspaper ignited immediately, and Bill placed a galvanized garbage can over the piece. This traps the smoke and reduces the exposed clay body black. The piece is allowed to cool somewhat in this smoky atmosphere so that the clay won't be reoxidized. After an hour Bill carried the finished piece into the fluorescently lit studio. See the results in color in Plate 35.

It so happened that around this time I was working on a piece of my own and found a perfect place to use the bird form I had seen Bill

Abright make. I incorporated it into my piece, and, wishing to acknowledge my source, I dedicated the piece to him by titling it "Bill's Bird Buys the Last Round." I sent him a note about it, and when I gave him a slide of the piece he reciprocated with a slide of the piece discussed in this essay, using the same form which he had titled "Harvey's Bird."

The point of this story is that none of us works in a vacuum. We are interrelated and borrow from each other for any number of reasons. As you develop your own style and ways of working, you use any techniques and materials that seem apt. Through this process you assimilate those images that are appropriate to you and your methods of working; the rest fall away. This was the only time I used Bill's Bird.

Showing Off: Photographing Your Work

by David Powers

When I started to photograph for this book, I had little appreciation for work done in clay, but I have come to regard it much differently after meeting and photographing the work of several dozen dedicated ceramic artists. Taking into account my own experiences as well as the countless slides I have seen that were taken by ceramic artists of their own work, I have decided to set down a few simple facts about photographing your own work.

What follows here are several good rules relating solely to taking color pictures of your pieces. First, present your work in the *best possible light*. In other words, photograph your work so effectively that the photos themselves disappear, in a sense, and the work is left to shine through in all its perfection. Anything goes as long as it works, and as long as you can repeat the process reliably for future shots.

Equipment

You don't need a lot of expensive, fancy equipment to photograph your work. The pieces shown in this book were photographed with either a 105mm, an 85mm, or a 50mm lens. I used a Nikon f/2 camera and a Sekonic L-398 incident light meter. I shot all the color photos from a tripod, which I feel is very important for obtaining sharp slides with good depth of field. For small pieces—2 or 3 inches in their largest dimension—I used Nikon extension tubes (the K-ring series), which slip onto the back of the lens between the lens and the camera body.

To recap: You need a camera, a meter (which may be built into the camera), a lens, a device such as extension tubes for getting close to small objects, and a tripod.

Film

I highly recommend using Kodachrome 64 slide film, for a host of photographic reasons. The technical aspects really don't make a lot of difference—it's the results that count. Kodachrome is warm-toned, has very high resolution capabilities, fine grain, and good color saturation, and is designed for making longer exposures than other films (up to one full second) without requiring filter compensation for the color shift that results from long exposures. The Ektachromes do not share all these characteristics, although they do have one major advantage over Kodachrome in the E-6 processing. Since the E-6 is not a proprietary process owned by Kodak, using Ektachrome frees you from having to send your slides to a Kodak lab for developing, and allows you to deal with a local color processor. (If you feel the need to know more about films, you can either write to Kodak (Eastman Kodak Co., Department 454, Rochester, New York 14650) or call your local field representative.

If you want to make prints of your photos to send out, slide film is still the best choice. The advent of positive color printing processes—Cibachrome prints or Kodak's own Type-R prints, both of which are now commonly available at most good color-processing houses—allow you to avoid the extra cost of internegatives, which always used to be a stumbling block in going from a slide to a print. In any event, when submitting photos for catalogs and other publications, it is common practice to submit slides rather than prints in almost every case.

My own preference is to shoot Kodachrome slides, have these slides duplicated on Kodak E-6 Slide Duplication Film 5071 (a marvelously tight-grained and color-rich film), and send the dupes out, saving the originals for the master file. In most cases dupes will satisfy any reproduction need, although if you have any questions about a special catalog or publication, speak directly with the gallery publishing the catalog, the designer doing the layout, or the printer making the color separations and doing the printing.

Since what you are really discussing here is giving yourself the opportunity to "show off" your work to people interested in what you are doing, it makes sense to establish a relationship with a good color processor who will be able to make multiple sets of dupes that you are pleased to have represent you.

Light

In this section I am only discussing shooting under daylight conditions. (This worked well for the photos in this book.) Daylight is "blue" in color, as you will discover readily enough if you use a tungsten film. Should you prefer lights, you can get photoflood bulbs that are balanced for daylight, or you can switch to tungsten film and get photofloods balanced to 3200° Kelvin, the same color temperature to which Kodak Ektachrome tungsten film is balanced.

Choosing the right kind of situation in which to shoot your pieces will take some practice. You want to shoot pictures in soft, indirect light, sometimes called "open shade." Harsh, direct light and the strong, deep shadows it creates tend to flatten the rich color characteristics of low-fire pieces. Softer light allows this color to come through, although in many instances the softer light has a blue cast to it.

There are several ways to make soft light work for you. The best is to work in a large, open, white-walled room with a nice western or eastern exposure. In this situation the light entering the room has a chance to bounce around the white walls and lose its blue cast. Always avoid shooting at times when the sun is entering the room directly.

Another situation that worked well for me while shooting for this book was to set up my backdrop in an open garage doorway, in such a way that the vertical part of the backdrop was in the deep shade of the interior of the garage at a time of day when the sun was not striking the setup pieces directly. I also shot pictures in the shade of a building after the sun had passed over its eaves, but this approach worked only some of the time. When shooting this way, the secret is to look at the sky. If it is blue, then you will get a blue cast to the slide, because the ambient light you are using comes, in part, from the light "bouncing off" the blue sky above. Generally the best time to shoot is on a day that is overcast (high clouds are ideal), because then the ambient light will "bounce off" clouds rather than blue sky. The resulting slides will have true color rather than the blue cast obtained under cloudless skies.

Often, when shooting in a room, you will have the opportunity to cross-illuminate your piece by placing it between two sources of light—for example, between two windows. This gives you the chance to shoot in a situation where there will not be a dramatic fall-off of light from one side of the piece to the other. It is perhaps the most effective natural-light formula, since you gain added relief on the off-side of the piece and you can thus show more detail and texture in your slide. Be careful here, though, because one of your light sources may be more blue than the other.

When possible in strong light (and this is a good alternative to using two light sources), you might use a reflector to bounce light back onto the off-side of the piece. Any large white surface can serve as a reflector.

With all this blue floating around, you can also obtain some filters that will help balance your color, and make it more accurate in your slides. Nikon makes an A2 filter (two units of amber) that is designed for taking pictures in the shade and balancing, or correcting for, the blue cast. Kodak's version of this filter is the 81A. On occasion I used two A2s together to balance for the blue, and though most photography lore says that you should not do this, I can say that it worked for me. You may want to try stacking filters in a similar manner to obtain similar results. The obvious danger in doing so is that you can fuzz the image quality. Let your experience be your guide.

Light Meters

Light meters—the very phrase sends shivers of apprehension up and down my spine—are, alas, all different, regardless of what you may be told. And I, for one, am very skeptical of *all* light meters. I don't trust them to produce the same readings from one day to the next. My eye, on the other hand, which always seems to me to be correct, has never satisfied me entirely either. This presents a dilemma.

Color films have very little latitude, unlike black-and-white films, so you must gear yourself up to go for the most accurate exposure possible with a minimum of $1/2$ stop, and preferably $1/3$ stop. I recommend testing your light meter occasionally, and treating it with kid gloves while you use it. Never bang it, drop it, or let dirt get in, on, or around it. You can test your meter in several ways to help

you ascertain its readings with some degree of certainty. My favorite method is to place a friend in the light conditions under which I will be shooting my pictures. I have previously made up a set of 3-by-5-inch cards labeled: -2, -1$1/2$, -1, -$1/2$, 0, +$1/2$, +1, +1$1/2$, +2. These numbers indicate the number of stops of over- or under-exposure I will give the slides during the following test.

I have my friend hold up each card in sequence while I run through the corresponding series of exposures, making sure that the card is visible in the frame as I shoot. I view the final slides on a light table, and choose the one whose exposure most closely satisfies my eye. The exposure indicated on the card held by my friend gives me an idea of my meter's accuracy. Complete this same test—using the same roll of film if enough pictures remain—with a piece of your work, first determining as closely as possible the light conditions under which you want to shoot. Use a piece that is predominantly white, and another piece that is predominantly dark, in order to determine for yourself whether the color of the piece will make any difference in your final slide. Take notes, and again choose the best-looking slide. Use this one as a starting point for shooting the rest of your pieces. Then, as you shoot, "bracket" your exposures—that is, shoot above and below your chosen exposure by increments of $1/2$ stop. Bracketing may seem like a waste of film, but having to reshoot something wastes both time and film.

Background

For the pieces in this book I almost always chose to use a black shooting background. I felt that this would allow the pieces to "float" on a kind of abstract field, and remove all visual data from the frame except the piece itself. Shooting like this works for the way I see ceramics. You may want to choose a different kind of background for photographing your own work. Whatever you choose—a white, black, or gray seamless paper background, all of which are available from photo-supply houses—you will need to experiment with at least one trial setup before you can establish your own shooting formula. You can also choose to shoot your pieces in a "natural" setting, in a gallery, in your studio, or whatever appeals to you. Just remember that the point of these photos is to show off your pieces. The less extraneous visual information you have in the frame the better your piece will appear, and probably the more direct your visual statement will be to people looking at your slides.

When shooting against a backdrop it is important to have no light strike the vertical "back wall." Light striking this portion of the seamless backdrop will only serve to attract attention to the wrinkles in it, and will destroy the floating sensation you want to create. For larger pieces, such as those on the scale of David Middlebrook's, it is important to set the piece far enough away from the back wall of the seamless to throw this wall out of focus. In such a situation a longer lens, such as a 105 mm, is especially helpful. And in this case, you also want to be sure to select an f/stop that gives a shallow depth of field, e.g. f/2.8 or f/4, but no higher.

Most good cameras have a depth-of-field preview button which, when depressed, allows you to get a sense through the viewer of how deep the focus of the image extends. If, when you push this button and look through the frame (the frame will get darker the higher the f/stop number you choose), you see that the backdrop begins to come into focus, you will know that you are shooting at an f/stop that is too small—that is, too high a number. (The higher the number, the smaller the f/stop, or the smaller the lens opening. The smaller the f/stop, the greater the depth of field.) Again, this is a situation that requires a little practice, and approaching it initially from the point of view of a trial run will take some of the pressure off you and will ease your almost inevitable attempt to take in all this photo-eccentricity in one dose. If your piece has a great deal of breadth to it, depth of field will be important in that it will enable you to

get all the elements of the piece in focus. The preview button will also be of help.

Miscellaneous

Here are a few items that might also be of interest to you as you try to make sense out of this whole problem of presenting your work photographically.

1. Should you find yourself shooting a piece so large that you can't find a backdrop large enough to give a solid field of color, you can simply mask out the extraneous edge information in the original slide by using an opaque tape such as Scotch Polyester Film #850, available at most art stores. Then, when dupes are made, they will show a totally plain field of background color.

2. The chances are that the more persnickety you become in your own work, the more persnickety you will become about the quality of photo work that is done for you. Establish a good working relationship with a professional color processor, and work with that person until your slide dupes are of a quality that satisfies you.

3. It is a good idea to have a rubber stamp small enough to print your name, address, and phone number on the border of the slide jackets. You can fill in other pertinent information about the piece—title and size and so forth—by hand.

4. Keep your slides together in a clean, dry place where the temperature does not vary too greatly. Kodak suggests storage at temperatures below 70°F and 45 percent humidity. Many people also keep their slides in plastic pages which have 2-by-2-inch pockets, or envelopes, on them to store each slide individually. These pages are manufactured by several different companies, and are available at al-

most all camera stores, and also through mass-circulation photo-magazine advertisements.

5. Remember, keep your originals. When sending out material, always send dupes. Also, consider keeping a record of which slides you send to which gallery, collector, or critic. In this way you will not only keep track of each of your slides, but you will also have a simple and straightforward means of knowing which clients you have been in touch with most recently.

The Flash

This section of *The Book of Low-Fire Ceramics* has been meant to provide you with a sense, in a very limited way, of what is involved in using photography to support your efforts to get your work out into the world. Building a portfolio of work is a very slow process, and you may feel that this technical stuff is better left to someone else.

As a working photographer I'm all in favor of spreading the work around. And yet, it seems pertinent to suggest that by doing your own photography you will begin to appreciate the importance of producing photos of your work that will let that work shine. The expense of the system I've described is minimal. It requires no lights, and accepts substitutes for certain elements. For example, your light meter may be built into your camera (TTL, or *through-the-lens* meter). Or you may use something other than seamless paper, such as a heavy cloth, as a backdrop. Whatever substitutes or ingredients you want to use in photographing your own work, bear in mind that 1) standardization of quality is a key goal in any method, and 2) you should give yourself enough time to work through initial mistakes. For instance, should you pull a commission piece smoking from your kiln, photograph it, crate it, and ship it off, and then realize that you have never shot photos in that particular way before, you may wish for a second chance when the photos turn out overexposed, or blue, or unsatisfactory in some other way. Take that extra time, or allow for it, at the outset. Kodak supplies one-day processing for slides in many regions, and three-day processing maximum in most others, even for slides given to your local pharmacy for developing.

Now you have it. Good luck, and keep the work coming.

Bibliography

Behrens, Richard. *Glaze Projects*. A Ceramics Monthly Magazine Handbook. Columbus, Ohio: Professional Publications, Inc., 1971.

Chaney, Charles, and Stanley Lee. *Plaster Mold and Model Making*. New York: Van Nostrand Reinhold Co., 1973.

Clark, G. Maynard. *The Art of Airbrushing for Ceramics and Crafts*. Los Angeles: Potluck Publications, 1975.

Fraser, Harry. *Electric Kilns*. New York: Watson-Guptill Publications, 1974.

Jorgensen, Gunhild. *The Techniques of China Painting*. New York: Van Nostrand Reinhold Co., 1974.

Kenny, John. *Complete Book of Pottery Making* (second edition). Radnor, Pa.: Chilton Book Co., 1973.

Kosloff, Albert. *Ceramic Screen Printing*. Cincinnati: The Signs of the Times Publishing Co., 1977.

Lawrence, W. G. *Ceramic Science for the Potter*. Radnor, Pa.: Chilton Book Co., 1972.

Lead Industries Association. *Facts About Lead Glazes for Art Potters and Hobbyists*. New York: 1971.

Nelson, Glenn C. *Ceramics: A Potter's Handbook* (fourth edition). New York: Holt, Rinehart and Winston, 1978.

Parmelee, Cullen W., and Cameron G. Harman. *Ceramic Glazes* (third edition). Boston: Cahners Books International, Inc., 1973.

Rhodes, Daniel. *Clay and Glazes for the Potter* (revised edition). Radnor, Pa.: Chilton Book Co., 1973.

Sanders, Herbert H. *Glazes for Special Effects*. New York: Watson-Guptill Publications, 1974.

Shaw, Kenneth. *Science for Craft Potters and Enamelers*. New York: Drake Publishers, Inc., 1972.

Singer, Felix, and Sonja Singer. *Industrial Ceramics*. New York: Chemical Publishing Co., Inc., 1963.

Taylor, Doris W., and Anne Button Hart. *China Painting Step by Step*. New York: Van Nostrand Reinhold Co., 1962.

Index